PRAISE FOR *VIRTUA MARKETING*

'To understand where VR will take us, as an exciting tool for marketing or more generally as an exciting new storytelling tool, it is important to learn about the technology and techniques. But more importantly, we have to place VR into a larger cultural context. Henry Stuart has written a must-read primer for anyone trying to understand the sprawling world that is virtual reality marketing, covering a whole range of other topics in the process.' **Anrick Bregman, founder and director at ANRK (New Realities VR/AR/MR), director at UNIT9 and former director at Guardian News & Media**

'Henry has written a must-read for anyone in virtual reality, marketing or anyone who is simply curious about the world of VR. Full of insight from the frontline, honest expert opinions and noteworthy case studies, this is an accessible, well-structured and informative book. Read it and you'll learn from one of the pioneers of VR marketing – a true authority in the field.' **Ashley Cowan, co-founder and CEO of VR City**

'In mid-2013, when Palmer Lucky's Oculus launched The Rift DK1, a group of creative post-production and film production companies (myself included) snapped one up; sensing that VR and 360 video could be the next frontier in marketing content and potentially provide a lucrative revenue stream. But for most, understanding how to craft engaging stories outside the rectangular frame and across a new 360 canvas presented challenges, previously unconsidered. A whole new toolkit of film-making techniques had to be tried, tested and developed before being able to go to market.

Not Henry. For him, the purchase of the DK1 was merely the next natural step in a journey he'd started as far back as 2006 when, as a photographer, he was creating 360 content for clients including *The Times*, Channel 4, BBC and the London Eye.

This headstart, fuelled by a natural passion for the format, enabled Henry to found his company, Visualise; one of the world's most respected and prolific VR and 360 video creators.

Henry – a kind, happy and friendly spirit – thinks, dreams and lives in 360. There is no one better suited, experienced or qualified to write this book. Anyone considering venturing into the world of VR and 360 video would be well advised to start right here.' **Simon Gosling, futurist at Unruly and 2018 winner of the Campaign Tech Award for New Tech Pioneer of the Year**

Virtual Reality Marketing

Using VR to grow a brand
and create impact

Henry Stuart

KoganPage

First published in Great Britain and the United States in 2019 by Kogan Page Limited

2nd Floor, 45 Gee Street
London EC1V 3RS
United Kingdom
www.koganpage.com

c/o Martin P Hill Consulting
122 W 27th St, 10th Floor
New York NY 10001
USA

4737/23 Ansari Road
Daryaganj
New Delhi 110002
India

© Henry Stuart, 2019

The right of Henry Stuart to be identified as the author of this work has been asserted by him in accordance with the Copyright, Designs and Patents Act 1988.

ISBN   978 0 7494 8286 2
E-ISBN   978 0 7494 8287 9

British Library Cataloguing-in-Publication Data

A CIP record for this book is available from the British Library.

Library of Congress Cataloging-in-Publication Data

Names: Stuart, Henry, author.
Title: Virtual reality marketing : using VR to grow a brand and create impact
 / Henry Stuart.
Description: 1 Edition. | New York : Kogan Page Ltd, [2018] | Includes index.
Identifiers: LCCN 2018029970 (print) | LCCN 2018030939 (ebook) | ISBN
 9780749482879 (ebook) | ISBN 9780749482862 (pbk.)
Subjects: LCSH: Marketing. | Marketing–Management. | Virtual reality in
 management.
Classification: LCC HF5415.13 (ebook) | LCC HF5415.13 .S8798 2018 (print) |
 DDC 658.80285/68–dc23

Typeset by Integra Software Services, Pondicherry
Print production managed by Jellyfish
Printed and bound by CPI Group (UK) Ltd, Croydon, CR0 4YY

This book is dedicated to my wife, Sue – thank you for your endless patience and support.

WIRED: What is your favourite definition of VR?
It's this notion – and this is very hard to express in words and I don't claim that I've ever succeeded in capturing it – that virtual reality is a future trajectory where people get better and better at communicating more and more things in more fantastic and aesthetic ways that becomes this infinite adventure without end that's more interesting than seeking power and destroying everything.

JARON LANIER, VR JUGGANAUT
See more at: www.wired.com/story/jaron-lanier-vr-interview

CONTENTS

ABOUT THE AUTHOR

 **Henry Stuart** is founder and CEO of Visualise, one of the world's premier virtual reality (VR) studios. He has provided VR content for major events including Wimbledon, the Olympics, and for brands such as Google, *The Economist*, Audi, Mercedes F1, FT, the BBC, O2, *The Times*, adidas and Ray-Ban. He is a regular speaker at events and has been published in *The Telegraph*, *The Independent*, BBC Online, *The Drum*, *The Guardian*, the *Financial Times* (FT) and Forbes. Since the launch of the Oculus Rift Headset in 2012, he has focused solely on producing VR and 360 content for marketing, churning out over 150 experiences for brands worldwide.

LIST OF INTERVIEWEES

This book is full of interviews with some of the most fascinating people in the VR industry, and this is who you can expect to find:

Jonathan Waldern (Introduction)

One of the pioneers of the VR industry, Waldern was responsible for virtuality in the 1980s and 1990s and was producing branded VR content while most of us were still playing with Lego! He has since gone on to set up DigiLens in Silicon Valley and is pushing huge innovation in augmented reality (AR). He shares some fascinating insights with us from this very unique perspective.

Anthony Ganjou (Chapter 1)

Head of Innovation and Technology at Chime/CSM, Ganjou is a hugely successful entrepreneur and innovation specialist. He has great insight into how brands can use VR and why VR is an important part of any marketing strategy.

Andy Corcoran (Chapter 2)

Head of UM Studios and Managing Partner, Creative Studios, Universal McCann. Corcoran works with brands to develop bespoke advertising concepts that grow their business. He has his finger on the pulse of the best new technology available for marketing and, crucially, understands when to use it. He is the former 'Head of Youth' from MTV and as such has valuable insight on how the next generations are using content.

Andy Hood (Chapter 2)

Head of Emerging Technologies at AKQA and President of the Cannes Mobile Jury, 2017. At AKQA Hood helps teams and offices globally to identify opportunities to innovate with new and existing clients, and to demonstrate the AKQA process and ethos of understanding, prototyping and applying emerging technologies to clients and consumers in order to solve business problems and create unique opportunities. Hood has worked with VR in some of the first and most ground-breaking projects for brands.

Stephanie Llamas (Chapter 2)

Vice President, Research and Strategy and Head of Immersive Technology Insights at SuperData Research. Llamas is perfectly positioned to give insights on all of the detailed information that has been collected by SuperData in the last year. SuperData has one of the most comprehensive sets of data on the VR industry available.

Richard Nockles (Chapter 2)

Another pioneer of the VR industry. Nockles holds two hugely important roles: Creative Director at Sky VR and CEO at Surround Vision, the VR studio. An award-winning writer and director, he has produced films for the United Nations (UN), SKY, BBC, Channel 4, as well as developing VR apps for a number of platforms and devices. Nockles is fascinating, candid and an all-round great guy to chat to about VR.

Ross Wheeler (Chapter 2)

Head of Automotive and Board Director at Imagination, Wheeler oversees clients such as Jaguar Land Rover, Rolls-Royce and Aston Martin globally. He was responsible for one of the most lauded VR activations for any brand to date – the launch of the Jaguar I-Pace.

Rohan Silva (Chapter 6)

Co-founder of Second Home, former Senior Policy Advisor to the Prime Minister and documentarian for the BBC. Silva has a deep understanding of emerging technologies and the effect they are going to have on the future ways we communicate, interact, play and learn. His knowledge and experience in the tech sector give him a unique position to comment on the future of VR marketing.

FOREWORD

The consumer content marketplace is cluttered and has become exponentially more so since the explosion of video on social platforms such as YouTube and Facebook over the past 10 years. Brands are constantly seeking innovative formats and need to stand out from the crowd or risk becoming invisible.

Well before Mark Zuckerberg launched his brainchild, marketeers were trying to reach consumers in more impactful, meaningful and memorable ways going back to the earliest billboards and signs on pavements outside shops.

Virtual reality has had a number of false starts going back many years, but the cost of production and also consumption has fallen dramatically even over the past 12 months alone. For the first time, brands can engage audiences in a far more emotional way, making them feel like they are present within a scene, rather than looking on through a window or frame. Countless case studies have demonstrated that deeper emotional connections drive empathy, retention and responsiveness like no other.

Virtual reality and 360 video also provide audiences with something that traditional video marketing has never really been able to achieve in a meaningful way – control. The format puts the user in control of where they look, for how long, and where they move next. This is incredibly empowering and fosters a deeper sense of brand loyalty. By adding on other senses such as smell, touch and haptics, brands can deepen engagement even further.

Over the past 10 years, I have worked with global brands to help them grow audience and customer loyalty through content. A business that I founded in 2012, Viral Spiral, was responsible for the management of what became the most viewed viral video of all time – Charlie Bit My Finger. I started Viral Spiral because I believed that user-generated content (UGC) would be a great avenue for brands to explore from a marketing perspective, given the empathy that one feels with videos that are more organic and less contrived. Although I couldn't have predicted that the UGC market would explode over the following few years, it did, and Viral Spiral was acquired in 2014.

Since 2016, I have been Founder and CEO of Blend Media, which has grown the largest catalogue of premium 360 video/VR content worldwide and the largest global network of professional 360 video/ VR creators. Our goal is to make immersive content easy for everyone, and we have already worked with many of the world's leading brands, agencies and publishers, including Intel, Google, Facebook and NASA. As we stand here today, in Spring 2018, it is difficult to imagine a more exciting industry to be operating in.

Global brands are making use of VR technology in marketing everything from experiences in cars to comedy 360 videos to wingsuit jumps or dives with sharks, to drive brand awareness and market their products or platforms in innovative ways. Using all of the common metrics, from click-through rates to dwell-time, the format is proving itself.

Of course creating 360 and virtual reality content is still not as easy as picking up a smartphone and hitting 'Record', but this book will guide you in great detail through the steps needed to do so, from initial project scoping, through storyboarding, production and on to the hugely complex and varied ways that VR can be viewed.

I have worked with Henry on a range of VR projects, from top music acts to whisky brands, and I cannot think of anyone better to act as your trusted guide.

It is surprisingly easy to make good VR content, if you follow some of the tips contained in this book. I also strongly recommend reading the industry overview, featuring interviews with some of the top characters and names in the VR industry.

Damian Collier
Founder and CEO, Blend Media

PREFACE

Thank you for picking up this book, which I am confident will give you a fantastic insight into how to ensure your virtual reality (VR) strategy reaches its full potential within your business.

So, a little background. Why should you read a book written by me? How did I get here and how can my experience help you?

I first started with immersive content back in 2005, when a friend showed me a 'Quicktime VR' 360-degree photo and I couldn't believe my eyes; a picture that you could move, choose where you looked. I was hooked. Already a keen photographer I started playing with creating my own 360-degree images, using an old DSLR camera, a fisheye lens and a Mac. I started Spherical Images in 2006 and entered the world of virtual tours.

I started with hotels and schools but soon picked up clients in the property world and other businesses that wanted more immersive ways of showing their premises and locations. In 2008 I shot a series of scenes for a computer game called Travelogue 360. This got me into some iconic locations around London and was the springboard for my next steps into immersive tech – gigapixels. You've probably never heard of gigapixels but they are coming back into vogue – it is a panoramic image that is made up from not just a handful of images but hundreds or even thousands. This means you can zoom and zoom and zoom.

I took my gigapixel system into St Paul's Cathedral in 2009 and, with their kind permission, shot the world's largest indoor photo at the time. This was picked up by the BBC and quickly went viral, being shared all over the globe. You could zoom in to the individual paint strokes on paintings on the inside of the dome! This established a relationship with the BBC and led to an opportunity that catapulted my immersive photography career forward – the royal wedding between Prince William and Kate Middleton in 2011.

The BBC managed to procure me the very best film and photography position of the whole day, on top of the Victoria Memorial, looking down The Mall in central London. I had a long view of the whole procession and all of the crowd and media crowded on either side. The resulting shot went viral in a big way and was featured and stayed on the home page of the BBC website for weeks after the event. I built a reputation as a specialist 360 and gigapixel photographer, and was picked up by Getty Images to shoot the London 2012 Olympics for the International Olympic Committee, becoming the first photographer to document the whole of the Olympics in 360.

It was around this time, in 2012, that I started playing with 360 video, as a natural next step in immersive content. I bought a camera built by Joergen Geerds, of the then fledgling Freedom 360 Cameras, which was made up of hacked-together GoPro HERO 2 cameras. It was all in a really basic-looking 3D printed case, which looked brilliantly like a school project, but worked like a dream! All of a sudden these 360 moments were not snapshots of time but were growing into stories.

It was, also, around this time that I met my future co-founder of Visualise, Anthony (Ant) Ganjou, who was running the experiential and guerrilla marketing agency CURB. Ant introduced me to the Oculus Rift Kickstarter project and we tried my content on the headset as soon as we could get our hands on one. It was a watershed moment for me – I was witnessing a whole new way of experiencing content. This was not just another way to watch a 360 video or still, this was a whole new medium, a whole new way to tell stories. Visualise was founded in 2013 off the back of this experience and we have not looked back since.

Since 2013 I have taken Visualise through the incredible hype cycle of VR (more on that, and Amara's law in the introduction!) and producing VR experiences for some of the world's biggest brands. Our work has covered the automotive trade, brands including Mercedes F1, Audi, Volvo, and the tourism sector, with Thomas Cook, South Africa and Mexico Tourism. We have produced films in Japan for *The Economist*, and 3D photogrammetry reconstructions of museums in Iraq and Syria destroyed by the Islamic State (ISIS). We have worked with the big tech giants that are most invested in VR, delivering projects for Samsung (with Lamborghini), Google (with the FT, Rotary and the Red Cross), Facebook (Van Gogh Museum) and Oculus (Harrods).

Visualise and I have contributed to a huge amount of press on VR over the years, being featured by the BBC, Channel 5, interviewed and speaking for *Wired*, featured in *The Guardian, The Times, Metro*, the *Evening Standard* and much more. I frequently talk on the subject of VR, 360 video and the future of the industry as a whole.

Through the years and the projects I have personally been involved in all of them, from their inception and initial talks with clients, through pre-production and planning, to being on the ground on shoots or briefing CG artists and developers. I have also spent my fair share of time at VR events, both industry and with clients, and seen how VR is used and the effect it has on the customer. I have seen when VR works and when it fails. I understand the pitfalls of activations and how to get more value from the content above and beyond experiential activations.

All of this experience and knowledge I have gathered over the years in the amazing world of VR is now collated in this book for you to build and learn from. Good luck and enjoy!

Henry Stuart,
CEO at Visualise

ACKNOWLEDGEMENTS

I would like to thank everyone at my publisher, Kogan Page, for their support and help in squeezing this book out of me! Thank you Charlotte Owen for holding my hand through the process and Chris Cudmore for your sage-like wisdom on refining the content. Also, a big thank you to Jenny Volich for the initial approach and for inviting me to write on this subject, which is so close to my heart.

Thank you to all of the fantastic interviewees that spent their precious time talking to me about VR marketing and opening up frankly about VR and their own projects. I feel really honoured to have you in my book – you have added huge credibility to these pages and introduced some brilliant new tangents to explore.

Above all, though, a huge thank you to my family, who have sacrificed countless weekends and evenings without their Dad/Husband. Sue, Annie May, Rosie, you are my sunshine, thank you for your patience.

An introduction to virtual reality marketing

Virtual reality (VR) is a technology in its infancy and this exciting new medium is only just starting to show its massive potential. From a marketing perspective it is an opportunity to immerse the customer in your product, brand, story or place in a way that is not just as good as reality but often far better. You have the ability to place people in the perfect version of your brand, give them the power to customize the product or choose how to experience this 'other' world.

From a marketer's perspective VR is a very exciting but also daunting opportunity. It offers unparalleled immersion and connection, with a truly captive audience and the ability to strongly affect people's emotions. On the flip side, the language for storytelling in VR is still being established, the hardware and array of platforms is confusing and there is also potential to make people feel physically ill!

The fact it is a new medium is one of the most exciting things about it; think about it, a new medium – a new way of consuming media, a new way of communicating with people, a new way to experience anything you could imagine! That is a hugely disruptive technology.

I have been working in VR since 2013, when I co-founded the VR studio Visualise. Before that I was involved in producing immersive content in the form of 360 photography, covering events for the BBC and Getty Images that ranged from the royal wedding in 2011 to the London Olympics in 2012.

At Visualise we have produced over 130 VR experiences. These have ranged from cinematic 360 films for the FT and Google through to fully interactive 'room scale' VR for *Wired*. Over the years I have seen the massive transformation of this fast-evolving industry and been on the coal face of producing VR marketing content for some of the world's leading brands and events.

In this book I am going to package up my learnings and pass on my thoughts on why VR is such an important part of the future marketing tool kit. I will also lift the lid on how we are making VR content now and how that is going to evolve in the future. VR is going to be huge, and part of daily life for billions of people – to put this in perspective, Goldman Sachs say that it will be bigger than TV by 2025.[1]

What is virtual reality?

There is the dictionary definition and then there is the definition that I think matters for marketers. In the future I could write this book purely from the perspective of marketing for content and experiences in a virtual world that is reached through VR headsets. However, that would not be reflecting the reality of the market in 2017. Right now VR marketing encompasses:

- interactive VR (running on game/real-time engines);
- cinematic VR or 360 video (more passive).

Interactive VR

This allows you to influence the environment you are in, it is dynamic. Interactive VR is best viewed on high-end VR headsets like the HTC Vive, or Oculus Rift, where a powerful computer can deliver a dynamic, smooth and immersive experience. Although interactive VR can also be used on mobile-based headsets such as the Samsung GearVR and Google Cardboard, the experience has to be greatly paired back in order to reach the required smoothness of the content. This often means that interactive VR is not chosen for entry-level, mobile-based devices.

Interactive VR can only be viewed on headsets – you cannot view it online (although WebVR is coming, it is early days). So how many headsets are there out there? According to SuperData market research there were just over 6 million 'premium' VR headsets sold in 2016 and 7.7 million sold in 2017. These are worldwide sales, so although not insignificant they are perhaps not enough on their own to justify larger advertising spend.

This means that the execution of VR activations on this part of the medium have to be for a very specific and intended outcome, ie you need to provide the headsets, the location and so on, and bring people to the content. In this sense, interactive VR is sitting firmly in the world of experiential activations, at least until headset sales reach a tipping point.

360 video

Also known as VR film, 360 video can be viewed in VR headsets and, crucially, online. This is getting the eyeballs on the immersive content that can justify the brands spending on the medium. VR films can both allow for high-profile experiential activations and reach large numbers of viewers through social platforms such as YouTube and Facebook. This is a vital point in this book. The reality of market constraints mean the vast majority of VR in marketing at the moment is 360 video.

VR and the hype cycle

VR is an emerging technology, as such you could view it on a Gartner hype cycle,[2] which is a visual representation of Amara's law (see Figure 0.1), coined by Roy Amara, that states:

> We tend to overestimate the effect of a technology in the short run and underestimate the effect in the long run.

Figure 0.1 shows an underperformance of the technology, which falls below public expectation, followed by an overperformance and impact of the technology, above public expectation. I think that VR is at the centre point of inflection of the curve, starting to deliver on its expectations. All of the hype of 2013, 2014 and 2015 has tailed off and the lack of patience and understanding of VR that we saw in 2016 and into 2017 is being replaced by an appreciation of the

Figure 0.1   A graph showing technology impact against time, aka Amara's law

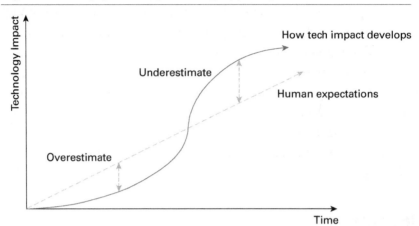

massive potential of this technology. I actually think that VR will grow to be bigger than even its initial hype suggested but I think it is going to take a few years to get there. I'm relieved that VR is now growing naturally, from its practical uses, and not just on a wave of excitement.

A lot of products don't make it out of their initial launches, if we are to look at another commonly used graph for displaying product uptake, Geoffrey Moore's technology adoption life cycle (Figure 0.2).

Figure 0.2 shows how a new technology is taken up by different parts of the population. Starting with the innovators, you could see this as people buying Oculus DK1 headsets from Kickstarter, through to early adopters, where we are now, people buying second-generation headsets. To 'cross the chasm' and have VR adopted by the early majority is the big challenge for VR now and this is where 360 video comes in.

360 video is a vital bridge we are using to cross the chasm towards mass adoption. With pure, interactive VR there simply are not the headsets out there to justify marketing spend and content creation from either brands or studios. From the brand perspective, 'not enough headsets so we will not make the content for it'. From the consumer perspective, 'not enough content so we will not buy a headset'. It is a classic chicken-and-egg problem.

Figure 0.2   Technology adoption life cycle

Technology adoption lifecycle

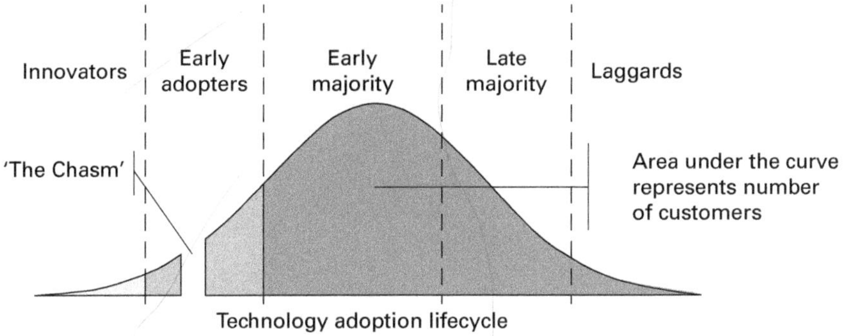

SOURCE Adapted from Geoffrey Moore's Crossing the Chasm (1991)

If content is created in 360 video, brands are able to have their premium VR headset experience and also reach the kinds of numbers of people they would expect from their conventional campaigns. This means investment in content that will in turn break the chicken-and-egg cycle. 360 video is not the future of VR – the medium will be so much more than that, but it is a vital bridge over the chasm on our journey to mass adoption. I will look further at the possible route to mass adoption for the industry in Chapter 6.

A potted history of VR

It is worth pointing out that VR is actually not that new. One of the first times that the concept was talked about was in a comic book in 1935 in the United States. The piece was called 'Pygmalion's Specticals' and it brilliantly illustrated a pair of spectacles that would allow the wearer to view another world (Figure 0.3).

[One of the next notable projects was Morton Heilig's Sensorama in the 1950s,[3] a piece so far ahead of its time that modern creative ideas with VR often do not push the boat as far (Figures 0.4 and 0.5). [Heilig's experience allowed users to watch content shot underwater, through a pair of lenses and have audio, smell and even a mist of water sprayed on them while they did so.]This style of VR experience is often (wrongly) referred to as a '4D experience',]the idea being that touch, smell and other senses add the extra dimensions of reality; 4D

Figure 0.3   Pygmalion's spectacles

SOURCE   Stanley G Weinbaum, Continental Publications Inc (1935)

experiences are common to theme parks or tourist attractions today but few of them combine VR headsets with the other senses, although this is changing fast.

Heilig did not stop there. In 1960 he went on to patent and produce (in prototype) the world's first head-mounted display, which he called the Telesphere (Figure 0.6). Check out the patents for this device and you will see it is uncannily like modern VR headsets. The headset had no tracking but did give you a stereoscopic (3D) view of a film, alongside stereo sound.

In 1968, computer scientist Ivan Sutherland and his student Bob Sproull created the brilliantly titled 'Sword of Damocles', a VR headset so heavy that it had to be suspended from the ceiling by a robotic arm, hence the name (Figure 0.7). This early VR system displayed simple wireframe graphics representing rooms and basic objects.

In 1984 Jaron Lanier founded the Visual Programming Lab (VPL) and launched a series of VR equipment that was, in its concept, far ahead of its time. Amongst these were the 'Eyephone' headset series

Figure 0.4   Morton Heilig's Sensorama, 1955

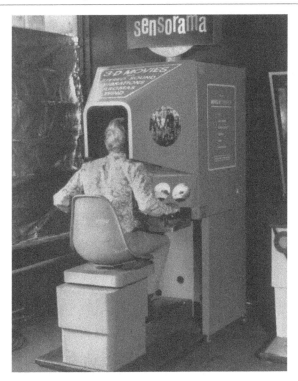

SOURCE   Reproduced with permission from the Heilig estate (2017)

and the 'Dataglove'. Lanier is often credited for coining the phrase 'virtual reality' – he's a fascinating character who has moved on from his work at VPL to music and to writing, notably the 2014 title *Who Owns the Future*. Lanier is alleged to be the inspiration for the main character in the 1992 film *The Lawnmower Man*.

The early 1990s saw the launch of the Virtuality Group and their arcade machines (Figure 0.8). These superbly retro-looking machines, possibly the most iconic of the 'first gen' VR devices, were actually pretty impressive! They boasted both stereoscopic (3D) viewing but also crucially a low-enough latency to reduce motion sickness. These devices could be linked together via network and multiplayer games played (Figure 0.9).

Looking back now, you could say that Virtuality arcades were the peak of the first-generation hype cycle in VR, with Dr Jonathan Waldern – in a brilliant video from 1994 – noting that his company was worth over 90 million US dollars.[4]

Figure 0.5   Morton Heilig's Sensorama, patent application, 1962

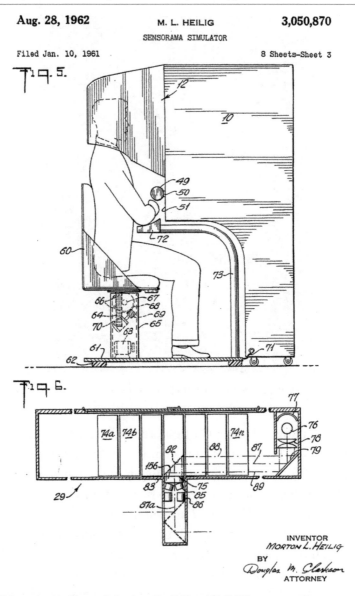

Aug. 28, 1962   M. L. HEILIG   3,050,870

SENSORAMA SIMULATOR

Filed Jan. 10, 1961   8 Sheets–Sheet 3

What followed was an industry that clearly did not manage to 'cross the chasm'. Sega and Nintendo both introduced headsets that had little or no commercial success, with their VR Glasses and Virtual Boy respectively.[5] Sega's VR Glasses were never released due to purportedly inducing severe headaches and motion sickness – an issue that

Figure 0.6 Morton Heilig's Telesphere, patent application, 1960

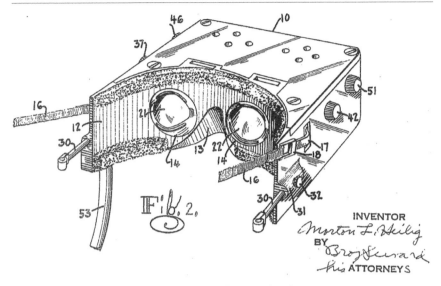

Figure 0.7 A head-mounted three-dimensional display, the 'Sword of Damocles', by Ivan Sutherland, University of Utah, 1968 (Fall Joint Computer Conference)

Figure 0.8   A page from the marketing brochure for Virtuality (by Dr Waldern/ Virtuality Group, Dr Jonathan D Waldern, 1993)

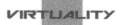

Head 4 Head Leisure System used in larger arcades, bowling alleys and theme parks around the world

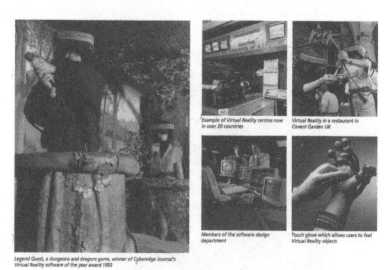

Example of Virtual Reality centres now in over 20 countries

Virtual Reality in a restaurant in Covent Garden UK

Members of the software design department

Touch glove which allows users to feel Virtual Reality objects

Legend Quest, a dungeons and dragons game, winner of Cyberedge Journal's Virtual Reality software of the year award 1993

dogged the early days of the second generation of VR. Nintendo's Virtual Boy (Figure 0.10) was released but after a short period was dropped; the reasons cited were a lack of comfort in terms of its design, a poor visual display with limited colours and, crucially, a lack of content/software.[6]

Figure 0.9   A page from the marketing brochure for Virtuality (by Dr Waldern/ Virtuality Group, Dr Jonathan D Waldern, 1993)

Throughout the 1990s VR started to trickle into our popular culture. *The Lawnmower Man* (1992) starring Pierce Brosnan was one of the most advanced films for its time. Allegedly based on Jaron Lanier's early laboratory days (see the fascinating interview with Brett Leonard and Upload VR[7]) the film tells the story of a VR researcher who uses his technology and drugs as a way of helping a simple-minded man, with disastrous consequences.

VR appears in *Red Dwarf*, 'Gunmen of the Apocalypse' in 1993 with Lester trying to experience sex in a 1930s film (and being inter-rupted). Then, in 1995, VR hits its peak in films, *Virtuosity*,[8] *Strange Days*[9] and *Johnny Mnemonic*[10] all coming out that year. *The Matrix* (1999),[11] took the VR concept to its natural extreme – a virtual world so convincing you don't actually know if it is real or not. This is ultimately where VR will get to, if the technology continues uninter-rupted on its current arc.

Figure 0.10 The Nintendo Virtual Boy

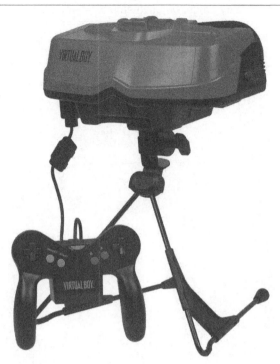

SOURCE Photography by Evan Amos (2016)

And then… nothing. VR failed to 'cross the chasm'. Until 2012 and a VR headset appearing on Kickstarter called the Oculus Rift.[12] So began the next hype cycle and our current, second (and hopefully final!) generation of VR.

Oculus was founded by Palmer Luckey, a 17-year-old living with his parents. He was frustrated that there was no affordable, low-latency VR headset on the market and so set about making one. With little more than phone components, solder and a huge passion for the potential of VR, Luckey's vision single-handedly launched the VR market as we know it today.

Early backers of the Oculus Kickstarter project included John Carmack and Brendan Iribe. Their backing and capturing the imagination of the public at large saw Oculus soar to being one of the most successful Kickstarter projects of all time, reaching nearly 1,000 per cent of its anticipated target!

Figure 0.11   The Oculus Rift CV1 Headset

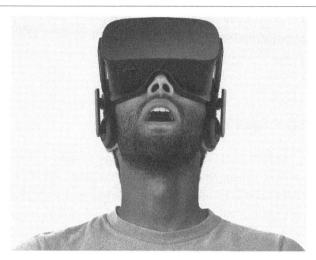

SOURCE Courtesy of Oculus (2018)

Carmack, who became Chief Technology Officer (CTO) of Oculus, is a household name in the world of computer games, being responsible for *Wolfenstein 3D*, *Doom* and *Quake*. He is recognized as one of the most talented programmers in the world and a leading mind in 3D graphic optimization. Iribe, who became CEO of Oculus, another game developer, was a user interface specialist who had worked on *Civilization* and had successfully sold his business, Scaleform, to Autodesk in 2011.

In 2014 Facebook bought Oculus for US \$2 billion, the first of the tech giants to move into this exciting new space (Figure 0.11).[13] Not to be left behind by their old rival, Google moved strongly into VR, announcing the Google Cardboard platform, created by David Coz and Damien Henry, two Google engineers, in their 'Innovation Time Off'. Widely seen as the gateway to VR, Cardboard allows people to fold a flat-packed, often literally, cardboard package into a VR headset that uses a smartphone as the screen. The vast majority of headsets on the market to date are Google Cardboard, with over 140 million shipped in 2016 and 2017 combined (SuperData, 2018).

At Google I/O 2016, their main conference, they announced a new platform, Daydream, building on the success of Cardboard. The Daydream platform also uses smartphones to deliver VR but is restricted to fewer, newer and more powerful, Android models. Since 2016, the main players have continued to evolve their headsets, bringing out next generations such as the Daydream 2 from Google and the Vive Pro from HTC. The headsets are getting better and better resolutions, tracking systems, audio systems and more – the rate of development of the technology is quite staggering. I will go into the market leaders and best options for marketing applications later in the book.

Will VR fail again?

Looking at VR's history you would not be blamed for asking if VR will fail again. So what is it about VR now that means it is here to stay? It frequently gets compared to other technologies that 'didn't make it' such as 3D. Well, the timing is right this time around. The convergence of technology, in a big part due to smartphones, has allowed for lightweight, compact components, high-resolution screens, gyroscopes, accelerometers and processor power, all to be packed into VR headsets at an 'affordable' price point.

Well, a lot more affordable anyway – to achieve anything like the kind of quality of VR we get from a mobile phone now, in the 1990s you would have needed to be at a university lab containing a computer in the hundreds of thousands of pounds. The ability for the smartphone to drive VR experiences is crucial – right now they are 'just' able to do this well enough; as the technology evolves, so will the quality of the experience and the uptake.

All things considered, VR is here to stay, although it is unlikely to have an uptake on the scale of the smartphone. It does not have the kind of immediate applications to daily life that something like AR does, but it does allow you to plug in to incredible experiences that are getting better and better at an increasing speed. From a marketer's perspective there is an opportunity to bring people experiences they would never have in daily life: Ralph Lauren bringing you to Centre Court at Wimbledon, Audi letting you drive the Nurburgring in their new R8, Peroni putting you in a scene from a 1950s film in Milan. These are all things that, as a consumer, I would love to do and things that are going to connect people more closely to brands and products.

The industry will get a big boost from a few upcoming pieces of technology – 'inside out' tracking and augmented reality being key ones. These are vital for the mobile-based side of VR to reach its potential and drive adoption. For VR to truly take off it needs the mobile experience to be as good as the tethered experience is now, and that's just a matter of time. With the launches of the Oculus Go and the Vive Focus, we are seeing the next generation of untethered VR headsets for the masses.

I would like to also add a point about the frequent comparison of VR to 3D: 3D is an evolution or adaptation of an existing medium – it is a way of viewing 16×9 content with depth. That content is based within a screen that we look at, taking up a relatively small part of our vision. VR is a whole new medium. It is not an evolution of anything else but an entirely new way of consuming content. You are in the content, part of the content, you are immersed somewhere and have power to interact, play, watch and collaborate. We have not even scratched the surface of what is possible in VR.

In Chapter 6, I will go into more detail on how and when I think VR will hit mass adoption. It's a long road, but we are talking about big changes needed in the way that people consume media and interact with each other. None of that is going to happen overnight.

A pioneer's view

I was lucky enough to talk to Jonathan Waldern, one of the pioneers in the VR industry. We spoke about his original company in the 1990s, Virtuality, earlier in this chapter. Virtuality was part of the first wave of VR and became one of the iconic pieces of VR equipment from my childhood. Jonathan has moved on to set up DigiLens, an AR-focused company, and is based in Silicon Valley. I interview him below on his thoughts on VR, its past, present and future – and you will see some fascinating insight from someone who has been on this journey before.

INTERVIEW

Stuart: I am absolutely fascinated by the early days of VR and the work that you did with Virtuality, it was just so far ahead of everything else.

Waldern: It was just too far ahead!

Stuart: It looks literally like the only thing that was stopping you was just that the technology was not advanced enough for the idea?

Waldern: That's right, that was the challenge. To round up all the componentry. We were writing operating systems for the graphics cards. We used to sit on the doorstep of Texas Instruments when they poured out their first samples of mass code processors so that we could do the real-time graphics generation. This was in the days when graphics cards were just starting to emerge. So there weren't graphics chips in those days. We very much had to shoehorn together all aspects of the low-level component technology to create an integrated system.

So it has always been the case, and to an extent is now, that the components are the critical aspect necessary to get the requisite low lag, high-performance and convincing graphics. All 3D depth cues and necessarily stereopsis and combinations of everything that you need to worry about to try and provide convincing immersive environments. That was very much the case and it became critically evident that the big hold-up was always going to be optics.

The key thing is not all the technology, though. Obviously, as you know well from producing content, it is the immersive sensation and the fact that you are there and actually in the environment interacting in the world. In AR, you take a step further because with all the SLAM (simultaneous logging and mapping) technologies and tagging, the ability to superimpose the object in the real world, it amps up yet again and it takes on in many respects more practical applications where you can merge data with the real world.

Just jumping out of the interview here to explain SLAM. This is essentially the computer or mobile device's ability to detect its environment and dynamically keep its position updated so that it can overlay content on to it or interpret that environment for something like automated driving. Waldern brings up a couple of terms like this, which are very relevant for the rest of the book, so I'll jump out and explain each one that you need to know!

INTERVIEW

Stuart: AR has the potential to be smartphone-like in its uptake and I think that VR is on a much slower burn.

Waldern: I think to a certain extent VR has even more challenges than AR. In so far as you have to completely synthetically create a realistic world and that puts a heavy emphasis on a very wide field of view, which also, you know as I say around here, with all these pixels to fill. That's when you get into the deep dive of higher-resolution capabilities and componentry. You know even with foveated rendering, which we work on here for our AR displays, you still have a steep climb. I think our approach is very much a step-by-step bringing through applications where there are already proven needs, and then expanding with AR into other areas, especially marketing and e-commerce.

Foveated rendering is another key term. This is the idea that you can maintain a higher resolution on only the exact area of vision that is being looked at at any moment, the other parts in the periphery of the view will be lower resolution and focus. In many respects this mimics how the eye works in the real world, and in theory means greater resolution at a lower cost in processor power and componentry.

INTERVIEW

Stuart: One of my theories is that VR is going to piggyback off the back of AR because I think once people like yourself have nailed the heads-up displays for AR then surely people can use those same displays, if they are wearing them day in day out, to take over more of their vision and create VR?

Waldern: That's exactly right. We're working on very wide AR displays just by switching all the crystal black and obviously making it immersive and providing a real-time VR environment. The back-end system and technology capability needs to be somewhat different, but other than that in terms of the visual experience it's the same challenge, just one is superimposing data on the real world and tagging it – and the other is basically creating a whole synthetic world where you don't have that challenge. I think the more advanced AR will merge into VR applications and vice versa – I think one universal place where we are superimposing data and merging the two worlds.

Stuart: Can you explain the difference between AR, VR and MR?

Waldern: I don't subscribe to the term mixed reality (MR), I think it is something that perhaps someone cooked up, as more of a marketing term to differentiate. I really think that AR pretty much describes the challenge. MR tries to differentiate in terms of SLAM and a need for an acute tagging and various other cues that might not necessarily be in AR. I think really that MR in that sense comes from the perception that AR does not allow for enough interaction with or immersion in the environment. It is more than just superimposing content on to surroundings.

Stuart: Looking at marketing and in terms of your original project, when you were doing Virtuality, was it ever used in marketing?

Waldern: I was recently talking to someone from a top marketing company in London called Imagination. Many years ago we did a joint venture between those guys, Ford Motor Company and IBM who were one of my investors and we launched the Ford Galaxy. At the launch show we had 12 custom VR systems lined up in a row and running this simulated ride. You could look around and see all the benefits of the car and have a virtual drive. You could interact with things, find out different features. The bottom line was you could learn about the car and take it for a drive right on the stand. So that was one example that we did, that was the first.

Another one we did was for Olin corporation who are, controversially, a gun maker but they do 'skeet' you know, like they use in clay pigeon shooting. We built systems for them that they took on tour throughout the United States, selling their skeet for recreational shooting and you could use a VR simulator to shoot skeet or flying ducks and things like that overhead. We did one project for Airbus, for trade shows where you could walk around the airliner and pick up seats, redesign the interior of the aircraft. Each time the pods were redesigned and coloured in a way that was in keeping with the brand.

We used to write all the content ourselves as there weren't any tools or anything like that out there, so everything had to be built from scratch. The Ford project was a multi-million-dollar launch, so there was a lot of money behind some of them. That was a keynote one. So I think that now, with things like AR kit and other interactive content development environments, we're going to see a plethora of opportunities there not least for promotion (experiential) but also thereafter to download so the consumers can get engaged more with the content and the products and look at them. People like Ikea are putting together whole catalogues where people can place furniture in their own homes.

I think it genuinely is going to become a preferred channel and you are already starting to see some top-name marketing companies purchasing smaller, more innovative companies that have typically been working in this area. Just like in the early days of the internet, they had a website, now they have to have their AR/VR website or AR/VR extensions to their website – all as part of their digital content and digital media strategy.

The key thing, obviously, is to have devices that are able to support this kind of application and provide a more compelling, more enthralling and more natural interface, something better than just holding a tablet or phone.

Stuart: Have you seen any of Morton Heilig's stuff from the 1950s?

Waldern: Was that the Sensorama?

Stuart: Yes, and he'd even patented something that looked unbelievably similar to the Oculus Rift back in the 1960s!

Waldern: I mean the Oculus Rift, well VPL was doing that at the same time I was doing it! The big old field sensors and the screen at the back, there was really very little innovation there at all. But when you've got John Carmack doing the graphics, the inventor of Doom, you've got Michael Abrash from Steam – when you get those two guys together, well I'm sure that took a different turn, they are very credible people. The rest of it was just ridiculous, a $1,000 PC and $500 headset does not constitute a consumer device. The tricky bit about consumer is getting under the $500 mark, all up.

Stuart: Well hopefully that's what the Oculus Go is going to do?

Waldern: Well that would be nice. I think there's some fairly fundamental things just in terms of resolution of the device and the ability to move electrons where you've got a 4000 by 4000 display, which is probably what you need. To move that kind of content in real time, 120hz-plus at less than 10 milliseconds, then you are up against physics and I don't think that conventional electronics will ever support that in real time.

Stuart: Do you think that VR is going to survive this time around?

Waldern: Oh my God yeah, VR is like water. It's a basic element. I think whether it's VR or whether AR it doesn't really matter. It's a desire, an innate human desire, to merge the digital world with the real world. Look at the world now, billions of people walking down the street, very often dangerously looking at their phones. The next step is obviously to merge that technology more empathetically with them, which is depicted in many movies and many shorts. What does this world look like when you truly merge those two? There will be devices that are much easier to use and more hands free, which no doubt many years from now will move into implant and various things that again have been successfully depicted by Hollywood.

So, I'm sure its all en route, but the bottom line is efficiency and the ability of mankind to operate more effectively in an ever-changing and expanding world. We're all thirsty for more knowledge, for higher performance in everyday life, more enjoyment etc. All the things that digital brings. So a more natural interface has always been the key. It's like moving from punch cards to teletype screens to graphics, tablets interaction, smartphones. Then of course, logically, wearable displays provide everything. It will become an inextricable appendage, it will truly merge.

Also, for driving productivity. Productivity is the fuel of mankind and productivity is what drives economies and drives people to beat starvation. There is an abundance of wheat today because satellites track harvesters, harvesters are now robots and you get stuff to market where things are tagged and things don't spoil. Whichever way you look at technology it has tremendous impact on everyday life. So there should never be any push back on the potential benefits of technological advance, which leads to greater productivity and a better life for everyone.

Stuart: I think people don't realize what the potential of virtual reality is and how big it is. As you say, people want to combine digital and the real world seamlessly. Essentially what VR will allow people to do is whatever their wildest dreams are, it's this ability to go into a world where there are just no limits. Depending on how it is structured, people will just be able to do whatever they want, and that is such a powerful thing. I mean it's such a powerful force for good as well but also for fun and for communication, everything – it's just about learning how to harness that.

Waldern: Some would say that books have been doing that very well since William Caxton, books and imagination! VR and AR are genuinely something worthy of an extraordinary amount of effort to bring to fruition. This will be brought through step by step rather than in a quantum leap.

What is VR?

The *Oxford English Dictionary* definition of virtual reality is:

> The computer-generated simulation of a three-dimensional image or environment that can be interacted with in a seemingly real or physical way by a person using special electronic equipment, such as a helmet with a screen inside or gloves fitted with sensors.[14]

Merriam-Webster defines it as:

> An artificial environment which is experienced through sensory stimuli (such as sights and sounds) provided by a computer and in which one's actions partially determine what happens in the environment; also: the technology used to create or access a virtual reality.[15]

Crucial to both definitions is the environment being computer generated and for that environment to be interacted with. This is where you get the argument for 'true VR' being those experiences that run on game engines, feature 3D graphics and allow for interaction.

360 video could not fit into this definition, as it is inherently non-interactive, a passive experience, like watching a film. 360 video is also not an artificial or computer-generated (CG) environment but either a capture of the real world or a pre-rendered CG video. For an example of a pre-rendered, CG, 360 video, take a look at Visualise's work for Inmarsat (a company that produces and deploys satellites).[16]

So if 360 videos don't fit into the above definitions then why are they such a big part of this book? The answer is firstly that 360 video is, in reality, the most effective use of VR for marketing if brands want to have similar reach to other, more traditional campaigns. Second, 360 video is evolving, with branching narratives, new techniques in breaking the fourth wall and an end game of volumetric capture and playback that will eventually converge with interactive or true VR.

360 video can be viewed in a VR headset, in fact, it is incredible in a VR headset. This is what leads me to consider it as VR, in all but a strict dictionary definition. You can feel transported and immersed into another world, be that real or imagined. This other world is all around you: if the video happens to also be shot in 3D then this world has a sense of depth to it; if the audio is captured with ambisonics then the sound is just like you would expect in the real world. I often use the term VR film interchangeably with 360 video.

With 360 video, on a VR headset, the brand has the ability to immerse the viewer in their world in the ultimate way to view the content. Then they can upload the same footage to web-based platforms such as YouTube, Facebook and Vimeo and reach millions of people.

On the second point, 360 video is fast evolving. Let's take branching narratives. Very simply this means giving people the ability to choose different outcomes in a 360 video. This can easily be compared to 'choose your own adventure' books. This simple tool allows interactivity to come to 360 video and begins the blurring of the lines. Next up are the storytelling techniques that are being used. One of the things that was noticed quickly by the team at Oculus was an effect that became brilliantly known as the Swayze effect.[17]

The Swayze effect was named after Patrick Swayze in the 1990 film *Ghost*, where Swayze returns to his loved ones after his death to try to help them, even though they cannot see him and hence he is frustrated and often helpless. This is a feeling that people can have in 360 videos when they feel disconnected from the scenes – like a ghost. There are techniques that have been developed to counter this – one of the most effective is being acknowledged by actors in the scene. This can be as simple as being looked in the eyes by an actor, or can go as far as actors talking to you. This simple action brings you into the scene and makes you feel far more engaged.

In advance of the launch of *Blade Runner* (1982), Oculus and Alcon Entertainment produced a piece of VR called Blade Runner 2049: Replicant Pursuit. This was a CG experience that allowed you to ride in a 'Spinner', flying between skyscrapers, through the dystopian world of the film in pursuit of a rogue replicant. The experience is CG but it is on rails (by this I mean you cannot control the spinner or your direction – all you can do is look around you and for a limited period put a 'lock' over potential targets). It is a headset only experience and without any real interaction, so by definition it is really hard to say it is true VR. But who cares – it is incredible, a perfect piece of advertising for the film that is enjoyed only on a VR headset. It is in all but definition VR.

So I would like to propose a new definition for VR in the marketing world:

> Virtual reality: a real or imagined environment that has been captured or created for either interactive or passive consumption on a wearable headset.

Where is VR going?

VR is going to evolve into something completely different to its current form. You will put a headset on and be transported into a completely dynamic, natural and limitless world. It will be an alternative world that we intuitively navigate and interact with. Technologies such as haptics – which allow you to feel, touch, interact in a natural way – will be the interface. You will not see the pixels on the screen; the audio will be a perfect, binaural, re-creation of real sound and you will feel at one with the content.

In this place you will be able to meet people, play, be entertained, collaborate, learn and so much more. This will be the 'Metaverse', a term originally coined in Neal Stephenson's sci-fi novel *Snow Crash* (1992). The metaverse will have its own marketing; out-of-home advertising will have another lease of life in the virtual world, but this time there will be no restrictions to billboards or physical issues such as cost or gravity. Perhaps you're familiar with Keiichi Matsuda's frightening look at the future of a life with augmented reality – *Hyper-Reality* (2016)?[18]

Who knows what this world will look like – if you say to any architect that they can build any building they want, with no limit to the type of materials, form, cost or time to create, then there will be some truly incredible creations. There will also be some horrors! Imagine if anyone can build a virtual building, anywhere – the landscape will be a mess, an eyesore. So there will have to be some kind of system or regulation, but who will determine this? What will the platform be that owns the metaverse – or will it be platform agnostic?

This little tangent should show you the complexity and scale of the unknowns in the future of VR and the creation of the metaverse. It is literally going to be the creation of a whole new world – and therefore a whole new platform for marketing. This may evolve like early cities growing on top of years of development, organically around the nooks and crannies of earlier times, or be shining new virtual metropolises on a rigid and policed structure of grids. Or will we even need 'buildings' with no weather or elements to keep out? In fact why build real-world structures or structures at all? Why not just beautiful natural vistas and parks?

What is special about VR?

VR can transport people to places, real or imagined, in a way that almost feels real. Unlike a film or computer game, where you feel detached from the action, in VR you feel a part of it. It is often described as the difference between feeling and seeing content. Essentially VR is tricking the mind, tricking your senses to thinking you are somewhere else. The better it is at doing this, the more convinced you are and immersed in this other world. Being fully transported and forgetting the real world, even fleetingly, is referred to as 'presence'.

From a marketing perspective this is hugely powerful – you have a truly captive audience that you can place anywhere and doing anything you want. It is an opportunity to give every customer the perfect piece of experiential marketing. Not just sitting on a set of *Blade Runner* drinking Johnnie Walker, but being in the police car, chasing a replicant and flying through the skyscrapers of futuristic LA.

Aside from the glitz and the glamour of experiences described above, there are real places and causes that charities have been able to immerse potential donors within. What is it like to live in a refugee camp in South Sudan? What kinds of issues are facing the people and doctors in these challenging conditions? The fact that you are standing in one of the patient's homes, looking them in the eye and hearing their story first hand is very powerful. When they look you in the eye, you feel like you are actually there in front of them. You feel a human connection, something completely unique to this medium.

The memories created in VR can sometimes be as strong and real as memories created in the real world. In Chapter 2 we interview Ross Wheeler, from Imagination, who describes feeling like he had sat in the Jaguar I-PACE and knew it like the back of his hand. Only on reflection, at a later date, did he realize he never actually had – rather, he had been in the virtual version.

Presence in VR

I'm hiding in a locker in a deserted spaceship, I'm terrified, holding the door closed with my hands, I'm peering through the slot in the flimsy metal door of a locker, staring at the alien that is stalking the room, looking for me! The alien turns towards me, the screen flickers, and a notification pops up telling me I have an e-mail, the spell is broken and I'm back in the real world, my phone buzzes in my pocket, must be the same e-mail. The sense of presence is broken.

Presence is a term derived from 'telepresence', which describes 'A sensation of being elsewhere, created by virtual reality technology.'[19] Barfield *et al* (1995) described presence as the subjective sensation of being deeply and naturally connected to the virtual world.[20] For the purposes of VR marketing, we can view presence as the complete connection of a customer to the world we capture or create – engrossing someone in the content.

There are a number of factors that lead to presence; I will detail these below, but it is important to note that presence is easier to attain in interactive VR environments than in VR films. Here are the highlights of the current thinking on what leads to presence in VR:

Key points

Michael Abrash spoke at Steam Dev Days in 2014, summarizing the research from the VR research team at Valve. This is what he highlights:

- A wide field of view (80 degrees or better).
- Adequate resolution (1080 pixels or better).
- Low pixel persistence (3 milliseconds or less).
- A high-enough refresh rate (>60 Hz, 95 Hz is enough but less may be adequate).
- Global display where all pixels are illuminated simultaneously (rolling display may work with eye tracking).
- Optics (at most two lenses per eye with trade-offs, ideal optics not practical using current technology).
- Optical calibration.
- Rock-solid tracking – translation with millimetre accuracy or better, orientation with quarter degree accuracy or better, and volume of 1.5 metre or more on a side.
- Low latency (20 milliseconds motion to last photon, 25 milliseconds may be good enough).

Abrash's 2014 list still stands up as the minimum factors you need for presence in VR. You could view these as the technology barriers to presence, most of which we have moved beyond now; however, some are still breaking the spell, most notably pixelation.

The highest, commercially available, resolution on the market, at the date of writing is Samsung's Odyssey and HTC's VIVE Pro headset with 1600×1440 pixels per eye each. This is a huge pixel density – you cannot see the pixels if you have this screen in your hand. It is only when you put two magnifying glasses in front of your eyes and then put the screen behind them (essentially what you are doing in VR) that you see the pixels. It is often one of the first things people say – 'Is it in focus?' 'I can see the pixels', etc.

Resolution has a long way to go until we don't see pixels in VR, 8k by 8k, rather than the approx 1.5k by 1.5k we have now will be needed. That's a huge jump and not one I would expect to see for a few years. Field of view is also going to need to jump up; currently the HTC Vive is 110 degrees – we should be looking for closer to 150 degrees, to eliminate the black borders to our vision.

There are some new entrants to the VR market, launching soon, that aim to tackle these issues, head on. Pimax Technology's '8K' headset is one of these (Figure 0.12).[21] Promising an eye-watering 8k resolution and, from the reviews and anecdotal feedback, it's very impressive too. StarVR has focused more on field of view claiming a giant 210° × 130° on the horizontal and vertical planes respectively.[22]

Beyond the technology though, there are more human factors that affect presence:

The physical environment in which you are watching VR

This is often overlooked but I think so vital. Are you sitting comfortably? Do you feel safe? Is the headset properly attached, comfortable, correctly adjusted, etc. Any of these distractions will mean you are pulled between two worlds – the real and the virtual – and therefore not getting the most out of either.

The ability to move with six degrees of freedom

For example, in any direction you want through a 3D space. This is where VR films fall short – pinning the viewer to one viewpoint,

Figure 0.12 The Pimax 8K Headset

SOURCE Image courtesy of PiMax VR (2018)

allowing them to look up, down and around them, but not to move left, right or forward of their own volition. If people try to move in this way, the virtual world will not react as they expect, breaking presence.

Seeing your own/another body

Often in VR you are disembodied, floating in a scene – one of the first things people do is look down and say 'I can't see my hands!' This is a presence breaker, so seeing your hands, at a minimum can greatly increase presence. At Visualise we wanted to experiment with creating true presence and built an experience with *Wired* called 'The Cell'. We used a hugely complex and advanced Vicon motion capture system to allow us to accurately record the body position of our arms, legs and head and therefore be able to see our own 'cyborg' body as we tried to solve the puzzles that allowed us to escape the cell. Once we had navigated the technical challenges of getting this hugely complex system working the result was absolutely fantastic, true presence in VR (see the result here: http://visualise. com/case-study/the-cell-vr-game).

Being acknowledged or noticed

A big problem in presence in VR films has the brilliantly dubbed title the 'Swayze' effect. Being in a VR scene, with life-sized, real characters around you playing out a story but being totally unable to influence the story or be noticed can leave you feeling like the Patrick Swayze character in *Ghost*, where he is unable to help his family and friends who cannot hear or see him – a real presence breaker. To mitigate this you can have characters acknowledge the user, saying things to them that don't need a reply, eye contact, or even asking questions that need to be answered. All of these approaches help to deepen your connection with the scene.

Interacting with the environment in a natural way

Having the environment react to you, in a way that you would expect it to, is important. If you try to pick up or kick an object and it does not move or it glitches and jumps in an unnatural way then it reminds you that this is not reality and breaks the sense of presence.

Social interaction

Richard Marks from PlayStation VR posits that one of the most important aspects of presence is being able to talk to people who are sharing the same VR scene. I have tried a VR experience from Oculus called 'Toy Box', when demo'd in LA at their Oculus Connect conference. I was sharing the experience with someone from Oculus and it was simply magic. Often the simplest ideas are best in VR and Toy Box is no exception. You are standing at a table with a host of children's (and not so children's) games all around you – catapults, dynamite sticks, lazer guns, remote control cars. In front of you is a rotating platform with various china pots and bowls that you can smash in any number of creative ways you can think of with the tools at hand. So it's fun already, but the amazing thing to me was that there was a floating blue head in front of me, with floating blue hands. He said 'Hi' to me... I thought it was part of the game and just said a cursory 'Hi' back, but he kept persisting, asking me questions and making suggestions to what I pick up and how I use things, etc.

It dawned on me that it was a real person! Real shock, wow! I started talking back and playing with him. One of the most amazing aspects was picking up a ping-pong bat and ball and hitting it backwards and forwards with him. The physics was perfect, there was no delay and I was chatting and laughing with this complete stranger in real time. Complete presence.

Using this book

This book is based on VR marketing now, an industry changing at a pace unrivalled in the history of technology. The evolution of VR experiences when compared to the evolution of film or gaming can be seen to be at light speed. Projects are built using iterations of technology that are changing on a near weekly basis, platforms such as Facebook and YouTube are introducing features such as ambisonics, 3D, heat mapping, and so much more. As such, this book is a snapshot of VR in 2018 and will no doubt have to go through frequent iterations to maintain pace with the market.

You will need to take the information I have learnt in this book, since my start with immersive technology in 2006, and apply your sector-specific knowledge to it along with any new movements the market has made. Advertising loves the new and there is no faster-moving industry than VR!

Notes

1 Bellini, H, Chen, W, Sugiyama, M, Shin, M, Alam, S and Takayama, D (2016) [accessed 11 February 2018] Profiles in innovation, virtual & augmented reality, Goldman Sachs, 13 January [Online] http://www.goldmansachs.com/our-thinking/pages/technology-driving-innovation-folder/virtual-and-augmented-reality/report.pdf

2 Gartner Hype Cycle [accessed 8 April 2018] [Online] https://www.gartner.com/technology/research/methodologies/hype-cycle.jsp

3 Morton Heilig [accessed 8 April 2018] The Father of virtual reality [Online] http://www.mortonheilig.com/

4 Dr Jonathan Waldern, Virtuality (1994) [accessed 8 April 2018] Talking about the size of VR and the potential of his product [Online] https://www.youtube.com/watch?v=2Imyn6QSq9s&feature=youtu.be

5 Brian M Engaget (2017) [accessed 8 April 2018] The Nintendo Virtual Boy reviewed [Online] https://www.engadget.com/2017/07/18/tech-hunters-nintendo-virtual-boy/

6 Langshaw, M (2014) [accessed 8 April 2018] Virtual Boy retrospective, Digital Spy, article on the demise of the Nintendo Virtual Boy [Online] http://www.digitalspy.com/gaming/retro-gaming/feature/a562419/virtual-boy-retrospective-nintendos-disastrous-foray-into-vr/

7 UploadVR [accessed 8 April 2018] Brett Leonard interviewed by UploadVR on The Lawnmower Man, August 2016 [Online] https://uploadvr.com/lawnmower-man-brett-leonard/

8 *Virtuosity* Film [accessed 8 April 2018] IMDB [Online] http://www.imdb.com/title/tt0114857/

9 *Strange Days* [accessed 8 April 2018] IMDB [Online] http://www.imdb.com/title/tt0114558/

10 *Johnny Mnemonic* [accessed 8 April 2018] IMDB [Online] http://www.imdb.com/title/tt0113481/

11 *The Matrix* [accessed 8 April 2018] IMDB [Online] http://www.imdb.com/title/tt0133093/?ref_=nv_sr_1

12 Kickstarter [accessed 8 April 2018] Oculus Rift: Step into the game; The original Oculus Rift on Kickstarter (2012) [Online] https://www.kickstarter.com/projects/1523379957/oculus-rift-step-into-the-game

13 Facebook [accessed 8 April 2018] Facebook acquire Oculus Rift, 25 March 2014 [Online] https://newsroom.fb.com/news/2014/03/facebook-to-acquire-oculus/

14 *Oxford English Dictionary* (2017) [accessed 8 April 2018] [Online] https://en.oxforddictionaries.com/definition/virtual_reality

15 *Merriam-Webster* (2017) [accessed 8 April 2018] [Online] https://www.merriam-webster.com/dictionary/virtual%20reality

16 Inmarsat Satellite Deployment 360 Video [accessed 8 April 2018] Visualise, 2017 [Online] http://visualise.com/case-study/inmarsat-outer-space-vr

17 Burdette, M (2015) [accessed 8 April 2018] Oculus Story studio blog, The Swayze effect [Online] https://www.oculus.com/story-studio/blog/the-swayze-effect/

18 Matsuda, K (1995) [accessed 8 April 2018] Hyper reality [Online] https://vimeo.com/166807261

19 *Oxford English Dictionary* (2017) [accessed 8 April 2018] [Online] https://en.oxforddictionaries.com/definition/telepresence

20 Barfield, W, Zeltzer, D, Sheridan, T and Slater, M (1995) *Presence and Performance within Virtual Environments: Virtual environments and advanced interface design*, Oxford University Press, Oxford, p 473

21 Pimax Technology 8K Headset (2018) [accessed 8 April 2018] [Online] https://www.pimaxvr.com/en/8k/

22 StarVR Headset (2018) [accessed 8 April 2018] [Online] https://www.starvr.com/

Virtual reality – why do it? 01

Virtual reality (VR) is a completely new way of engaging with people. It is a new way of telling stories and transporting people to other worlds. It is able to give people the experience of doing or feeling something like they were actually somewhere else. Mark Zuckerberg rather cornily called it a teleportation device – he wasn't far off. In this chapter we look at why this new medium is an important, and fast becoming essential, marketing activity.

Here is an interview with Anthony Ganjou, actually my co-founder at Visualise, although he now focuses his time on his role at Chime/CSM, as their Head of Innovation and Technology. Ant founded the experiential and guerrilla marketing agency CURB in 2008 and went on to sell it to CSM, the global sports marketing group, in 2016. His first client was the US President Barack Obama and through CURB he reached revenues of £11 million before its sale. He is an incredible mind in marketing and technology, and opportunities to meld the two, so is perfect to explain the question – why do virtual reality?

INTERVIEW

Stuart: Broadly speaking, why should you do VR in marketing?

Ganjou: The key reason is that it is the most immersive, engaging and interactive content channel in the world. It fundamentally allows you to put people at the heart of your brand and marketing communications, in a way that no other channel does. It's about allowing you to curate and create an environment that totally encompasses the customer's every sense.

Stuart: How do you see the relationship between experiential marketing and VR?

Ganjou: Experiential marketing is all about customers experiencing a brand or product physically – immersing the customer in your brand so they feel a part of it, helping them understand the brand story or more deeply understand a product offering. What VR is doing is making it easy to transport customers into an environment where you can tell them that story in a more powerful way than any other medium. You can't replace reality, but you can bring the rainforest to the middle of Westfield Shopping Centre for L'Oréal! The customer will feel what it is like to be part of your brand, your values, your vision. It is creating an easy bridge to transport your customers to the environment you want them to experience – this is often in public places at the moment, but more and more often this is from the home, allowing experiential activations for brands to be anywhere!

Stuart: How does VR sit in the 'content marketing' world?

Ganjou: Driving engagement through content marketing is everything for brands, VR is able to get huge cut-through in this space. When VR came about, it was seen as a novelty, something interesting and new, something that captured people's imagination in a way that no other content channel could do. Fundamentaly, because of the very nature of how immersive it is, you are putting someone into an environment where they can see everything and anything that you want them to see. It is a completely different experience from a 2D or 3D content channel. What that means is that you can immerse them much more intimately into your marketing and communications plans.

Stuart: What about first mover advantage? Is VR still a novelty?

Ganjou: I think it is getting to the point now where the hardware that is used, by that I mean everything from headsets to bodywear to engagement sensors to extra-sensory elements, is only getting better and better in every single way imaginable. So whilst there was a sense of novelty, thanks to the huge consumer press and general interest in VR around just putting a headset on and looking at another world or time, we're moving beyond that novelty. We're seeing major multi-billion-dollar manufacturers investing huge funds in hardware that makes the experience multiples better than it was when VR first started.

So we're moving to something now that is wildly more immersive or valuable than it could ever have been back in 2013/2014. The nausea issues have been worked through, the resolution is getting really good, the power of the headsets and devices that power them is improving exponentially too. The rate at which the hardware is evolving, and making a much more intimate, true and real virtual experience is driving the industry beyond being a novelty to being a unique content medium to help brands engage with consumers.

We have moved beyond the time you can do virtual reality for virtual reality's sake. I think the opportunity now for brands is to look very carefully about what virtual reality can do. It can be used as a tool to really bring to life your brands, bring to life your marketing and communications, it's about being clever and strategic about how you're using it. Not just using it because it is virtual reality.

Stuart: Do you think it is difficult to activate in VR?

Ganjou: I think VR presents an entirely new set of challenges, from production, to creative storyboarding, to the way in which the consumer physically experiences it, to the distribution of the content and the measurement of return on investment (ROI), which are challenges created because VR is entirely different from any other existing content channel. The reality of what you are seeing is hundreds of different stakeholders in the VR landscape, be they content producers, agencies, advisers, directors, experiential agencies, hardware manufacturers, software manufacturers that are trying to make it easier for brands to navigate that landscape.

In the same way that the hardware is evolving to make a much more true and extraordinary VR experience, the number of stakeholders in the industry that are helping clients navigate the landscape, produce good VR and capture long-term value from VR is increasing as well. I think now, more than ever, that clients have access to hundreds of different brilliant stakeholders involved in the industry, who can help easily and efficiently to navigate the journey of VR production and ultimately activation.

Stuart: Which industries are going to benefit most from VR?

Ganjou: Any industry where immersing a consumer in a brand environment is beneficial is going to be a candidate for VR, it is that broad. Hotel brands, automotive brands, attractions, theme parks, brands that fundamentally have content they want to bring the consumer closer to, Disney for example. There is also such rich territory in rights-driven ownership too – look at sport, something that normally lives and breathes in 2D can be re-created or captured in 360 and pulled into VR.

In sport, being able to put the fan closer to the experience, or even in the middle of the experience and allowing them to feel like they are part of the experience, is a huge thing for sponsors, rights owners and brands alike. The possibility for 'money cannot buy experiences' for fans is massive. You can capture a goal from within the net and let the viewer watch it like they were there; you can create experiences of training with the players, allowing you to feel like you're meeting and playing with your biggest idol. This is great brand association and will build strong connections with consumers.

Sure, there is also the potential for completely live sporting events, which would fall into the entertainment bracket, rather than marketing, but the potential supporting content and experiences in VR for existing campaigns is absoluetly massive. F1 is another example – put people in the pit lane as the mechanics change the wheels and fill up the car, put fans in the thick of it – who wouldn't want to see that!? Again, it's an extrodinary and unique perspective that people would otherwise never get.

Stuart: What do you think are the next steps for the VR industry?

Ganjou: I think we're at the dawn of what VR is going to become. The next decade is going to change the way that VR is delivered and consumed. You only need to look as far as what The Void is doing in Westfield with *Star Wars*, that once you start to add haptic elements, sensory elements, experience-led elements, motion tracking-led elements, then you see that the scope of producing extraordinary experiences for brands is literally limitless!

So I think the brands that recognize this is a nacent industry, and the way the technology across the board is advancing, to make virtual reality more immersive, more engaging, more real and bringing brands closer to consumers, those are the ones that are going to capitalize on the huge potential of virtual reality. The next 10 to 20 years is going to define the way brands produce virtual reality and the way in which consumers experience it, to the point where it becomes far beyond what it is currently in terms of an immersive and engaging experience.

Stuart: How big do you think VR is going to get?

Ganjou: It is going to become one of the key and ubiquitous channels for how people experience branded content. I don't think we're ever going to see it overtake television, I don't think we're ever going to see it overtake how people experience content on mobile or tablet devices. I do think that as a content channel, the scale and scope of the market is going to be double digits from where it is now, in terms of ad revenue spend, the numbers of people using it globally. It's here to stay, it is only going to get better and better.

I think the way that brands work out how they can use it and embed it in the fabric of everyday lives of consumers is going to define its growth. With the rate of growth of the industry, it is going to become more prevelant and more embedded in the day-to-day life of us as consumers.

Strategic benefits

Closer brand connection

VR and experiential marketing

Experiential marketing has boomed over the last few years, fast taking spend from broadcast or media. At its heart, experiential allows consumers hands on with products, gives them amazing moments they associate with a brand and allows a rare cut-through from traditional advertising. Customers are getting better and better at ignoring adverts, the result of years of bombardment. So building a unique area to demonstrate a product can result in far more traction and ROI than a traditional billboard, for example.

A brilliant example of some experiential was the Blade Runner 2049 Experience at Comic-Con in San Diego. This was a perfect re-creation of a bar scene from the iconic film, allowing fans to feel like they were in the movie. You could have some sushi, avoid the LAPD scanning for replicants, see costumes and props from the film and, crucially, you can sit at the bar and order some Johnnie Walker. So people have had an amazing experience, they have probably taken a lot of photos, posted and shared them and they have tried a brand's product in a highly charged emotional state. Sure, the number of people who would have experienced this would be less than could see a billboard on a busy highway, but which is going to generate more engagement and more buzz?

VR is both an evolution of experiential and a vital part of current experiential. Take the example above of Johnnie Walker's Blade Runner Experience – you have walked around the set and had actors come up to you, felt a part of the scene, but there is only so far that this can take you. Well, there was another part to the experience, a VR activation: people were invited to sit on a series of specially made chairs and put on headsets (Samsung Gear VR), then they were flying the 'police spinner' (flying car) through the skyscrapers of futuristic Los Angeles.

This addition of the VR component, to the larger experiential as a whole, allowed the punters to contextualize the whole event.

The VR gave them a thrilling ride but also a story that they felt part of. The headset was only playing content for them, they were flying the car – so when they take off the headset and see the crashed Spinner in front of them and the police and characters around, they can start interacting in a natural way.

The US brand Toms has a very unique message: buy a product and the company will help a person in need. People wanted to see some of the people benefiting from this brilliant initiative, so Toms captured VR films of some of the children they had helped in Peru, Guatamala and Cambodia. With VR they could transport people from their stores to the children they were helping, opening the eyes of their customers to the real impact they were having on other people.

So VR can allow experiential activations to dive deeper, immerse customers in another world in a way that is personal and captivating. There is no more captive audience than someone in a VR headset, they literally cannot look at anything else!

The evolution of experiential

In its essence, experiential is allowing customers to feel and interact with product, rather than just passively observe it. VR will allow this to happen anywhere, it can take experiential into the home. Why shouldn't you put on a headset and be in the bar from *Blade Runner*, while sitting at your kitchen worktop? You could do this on a Google Cardboard headset with your own phone, the headset could have been a free giveaway when you bought your bottle of Johnnie Walker.

Right now, doing this kind of activation would be most practical as a 360 video, as you can get this content on to older phones and it plays well with Google Cardboard. Look to the future though. In a few years' time, we will be able to interact with the bar staff, talk to people in the scene and even be in there with our friends who you can also see in the scene, represented by different characters from the film. That is a hugely powerful opportunity for brands. The only thing stopping this from being a reality right now is adoption. As soon as there are more premium headsets out there we will all be experiencing stunning, memorable moments, brought to you by... insert brand here!

First mover advantage

VR is still a novelty. The vast majority of people you bump into on the street would not have tried it. Whilst this is a bad reason for doing a VR piece, in isolation, the novelty factor must be considered. People will see others in a headset and are often drawn to see it for themselves. This effect can be maximized by showing a second screen with the view of the person in VR on it. If it is something dynamic and exciting then people will want to try it for themselves.

As VR is still so novel it often means that it may be the first time a particular industry or niche has used it, meaning great PR potential. We've seen countless experiences amplified by great press coverage. One of our biggest successes, with zero PR spend, was *Walk With Penguins*,[1] a film we made about endangered penguins for the charity BirdLife (Figure 1.1). This was the first time the press had a nature documentary in VR that allowed people to get so close to the animals. The result has won countless awards and was featured in the *Independent*, *Express*, on *The Gadget Show* and more.

Impact

VR has 'cut through' – it is deeply memorable, able to powerfully stimulate emotion and transport people to other worlds, real or

Figure 1.1 A screen grab from *Walk With Penguins*

SOURCE Visualise (2017)

imagined. VR is able to have such impact as it is essentially fooling the senses, it is taking over two of the most powerful ways we interpret our environments, sight and sound.

VR has three very special properties that make it so powerful for marketers:

- It is transportive.
- It is human.
- It is memorable.

Transportive

Virtual reality is often described as a 'teleportation device' – you put the headset on and are transported to another place, real or imagined. From a brand's perspective this is an opportunity to completely immerse clients in the perfect brand experience. Essentially it is an opportunity to blend the best of film, game and experiential advertising into one moment. Imagine those glossy TV adverts we all grew up with, but only this time you are in the advert, sitting on that Riva boat off the Amalfi coast of Italy, drinking a Peroni, or being passed chewing gum by the Wrigley's girl. Really good VR transports you so convincingly that you even forget the real world sometimes and are completely engaged in the virtual. This feeling is called 'presence' – an important term in VR that we will speak more about in this book.

Human

A broad term, but in the context of VR I am looking at the ability of content to affect people emotionally and physically. VR is often touted as a great 'empathy device', hence its great success with charities. In a VR film, if you are standing close to someone and can see the whites of their eyes as they talk to you, you get a very similar feeling as if the person was actually standing there. If they get too close you want to step back, the effect of someone entering your personal space. A great example of this is our work we did with Médecins Sans Frontières (Doctors Without Borders);[2] in the headset you are transported into some of the most challenging places in the world to live – refugee camps in countries affected by war and poverty. You stand in the houses of patients, sit around their tables with their families while they eat and sing, and you hear their stories, from them, in their company. This is incredibly powerful and has led to a hugely successful campaign of fundraising. I'll touch more on this and the huge success the UN experienced later in this chapter.

Memorable

Home to some of the most unflattering pictures in technology on the web, the tech-loving man with his mouth open and a black lunch box stuck over his eyes! But if you look again, there is something in common in all these shots – people are totally absorbed and amazed. People remember, talk about and want to share their experiences in VR. It's the ultimate 'lean forward' medium, allowing for a truly captive audience.

If the VR is really good, and you have a sense of presence, then you may well remember the experience, not for its novelty but for the practical application of the content in the headset. The most memorable VR experience I have ever had was thanks to Industrial Light and Magic and Lucas Film at 'The Void' – their incredible, immersive, team-based shoot 'em up based in the *Star Wars* galaxy. It really made me think I was in one of the films, and was thrilling and truly memorable – a taste of things to come.[3]

Visualization/authenticity

One of the things that often stops people purchasing a product or service is their lack of ability to 'visualize' what that experience is going to be like. VR can take away the buyer's fears by showing people quite literally what they will be getting. One example is our work with the travel agent Thomas Cook.[4] In the UK in 2015, we shot a series of five-minute films in New York, Singapore, Cyprus, Egypt and more that allowed people to preview a holiday before deciding to buy (Figure 1.2). This led to a massive uplift in sales of those holidays (see section on ROI below).

Lowe's department store in the United States in 2015 built a series of 'holorooms' that allowed customers to place different items of Lowe's furniture in virtual rooms,[5] the idea being that if people can see how the furniture will look, in situ, then they will be more likely

Figure 1.2   Screen grab from Visualise's Thomas Cook VR experience over New York (2015)

to buy. It is something that Ikea has since taken to its natural next step, in augmented reality, allowing users to place virtual Ikea furniture in their own homes![6]

This can also be looked at as authenticity. VR is an inherently honest medium, particularly if you are capturing the real world. We shot a 360 advert for Waitrose in 2017 that took this to its extreme.[7] Waitrose was running a series of TV ads that showed footage from its actual farms: chickens running out of their hutches, even an action cam on a cow's collar as it fed. Adam and Eve DDB, the creative agency, proposed that the next advert was captured in both TV, 16×9, format and, at the same time, in 360. So people could see, by simply turning around, that the view they had on TV was not studio shot and was a real place. The shot we did this with was tuna fishing in the Maldives (Figure 1.3) – nice gig you may think, unless you're stuck in the sweaty bows of a tuna boat 24 hours a day, seven days a week, looking for tuna!

Preparing for the future

There is no doubt that VR will be a part of the future media landscape; the question is more when than if. As such, companies and

Figure 1.3   Screen grab from Visualise's Waitrose VR experience (2017)

brands are experimenting with VR in order to learn the techniques involved in effectively telling stories and bringing customers on journeys in this new medium. If a brand can establish a series of content and a language for connecting with consumers now, in VR, then they will be far ahead of the competition and ready to move fast and effectively when consumer VR, en masse, becomes a reality.

Return on investment (ROI)

It is all well and good talking anecdotally about the impact of VR, but what about actual figures? Here's some of the highlights from Visualise and the industry at large.

Thomas Cook – Try Before You Fly

In this project we captured the perfect day for a tourist in New York, including a helicopter ride over Manhattan. Back in the UK, Thomas Cook presented this experience in their flagship stores and allowed customers to take a virtual tour of New York. The result – a 190 per cent uplift in sales when people previewed the holiday in VR.

The British Army – Recruitment

We captured point-of-view (POV) experiences of climbing, tank driving, parachuting and even combat training for the army. These were built into an app for the Samsung Gear VR and taken on the army's recruitment drive all over the UK (Figure 1.4). They found that on the days they used the VR experience they received 66 per cent more recruits.[8]

Financial Times – Hidden Cities, Rio

This documentary takes you into the favelas of Rio de Janeiro in the run-up to the 2016 Olympic Games and explores how gentrification is changing them and the issues at play in this fabulous city (Figure 1.5). The FT has said that this is their most successful video of any format with an average dwell time of 2.30 minutes and a 0.2 per cent bounce rate.[9]

Clouds Over Sidra – Within

Clouds Over Sidra was the first of the refugee-empathy VR films. It showed the power of VR for telling meaningful stories and putting the

Figure 1.4   Screen grab from Visualise's British Army Recruitment VR Experience (2015)

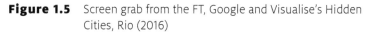

Figure 1.5 Screen grab from the FT, Google and Visualise's Hidden Cities, Rio (2016)

audience in other people's shoes. Shot by Within, the film premiered at the World Economic Forum in Davos, Switzerland. It was screened at a high-level donor meeting prior to the Third International Humanitarian Appeal for Syria in Kuwait in March 2015, which eventually raised $3.8 billion.[10]

After its initial launch it was brought to Canada for the Toronto film festival in 2016 and toured Mississauga, Ottawa and Vancouver. The resulting viewings showed the following stats from a total of 95 events: over 7,000 people were able to experience the project at 29 public screenings, 38 private screenings and 29 schools.[11]

The Sidra Project found the following results from this phase:

- 95 per cent of people surveyed agree that the Sidra Project 'heightened their sense of empathy towards the plight of refugees'.

- 87 per cent are more motivated to help with efforts for refugee resettlement in Canada.

- 73 per cent have taken action in one form or another to help with the refugee resettlement efforts in Canada.

- 94 per cent believe the project would build more support for refugees if more people experienced it.

This film is largely credited with the explosion in charity VR projects or 'empathy VR'.

Google's research

On the Google website 'think with Google' they explore the question 'Is 360 Video Worth It?'[12] Google ran a split test, with an experimental campaign for Columbia Sportswear. They wanted to find out if 360 video advertising drove more engagement than standard video advertising. So they made the same advert in normal video and in 360 video. The results were fascinating – they are taken here directly from the report:

Key points

1 *360 video doesn't overperform on traditional viewer metrics.*
Surprisingly, the 360 in-stream ad underperformed the standard ad on view-through rate, across desktop and mobile. This led us to conclude that viewers aren't always in the mood to interact with 360 video if they are primarily watching standard video.

But, interestingly, we found that 360 ads made up for this with other strengths.

2 *360 video motivates viewers to watch more and interact.*
The 360 video ad had a lower retention rate than the standard ad. But, the 360 ad also had a higher click-through rate, meaning that viewers were more interested in checking out the full-length version of the video. So, as a promo for the longer video, the 360 version of the ad worked extremely well. Viewers didn't even need to watch the full cut to know they wanted more.

The interaction rate, which measures how often viewers explored the 360 functionality by tilting or scrolling, was higher than the view-through rates for the 60-second 360 ad. This means that the 360 ad drove engagement via interactions, even if people didn't watch 30 seconds or more.

3 *360 video drives viewers to share, subscribe and view other videos.*
The 360 ad trounced the standard ad on all the earned action metrics, including views, shares and subscribes. In total, the 360 ad drove

41 per cent more earned actions than the standard ad. It also drove more engagement with Columbia's YouTube channel than the standard ad.

But it gets even more interesting: since we kept the 60-second ads and the full-length pieces unlisted for the duration of the experiment, the only way a viewer could get to a longer piece was to click from the ads. So, we expected the views for the longer 360 piece to match the clicks for the 360 shorter ad... but they didn't.

This means people who saw the longer 360 piece were copying the URL to share directly with others. In fact, we saw messaging apps like WhatsApp and iOS messenger listed among the traffic sources for the 360 version – but not for the standard version. The full-length 360 video had a 46 per cent higher view count at the end of our experiment than the standard full-length piece. As a result, the 360 ad was a more efficient buy since its cost-per-view was lower when organic and paid views were combined.

The crucial result of this study by Google was the massive increase in engagement, shares and interaction over standard video. Ultimately being shared 46 per cent more than the standard equivalent video is a ringing endorsement for the medium.

Omnivirt research

Omnivirt, the VR/AR advert platform, has run a study on over 1,000 ad campaigns to benchmark performance metrics and engagement in the industry. Admittedly this is focused more on online usage and therefore not headset but this is still very important for VR producers – as the reality now is that more people are seeing VR content in this way.

Their findings show that using 360-degree content compared to traditional content gives a click-through rate increase of over 300 per cent! There are a number of other stunning metrics that you can find by following the link given in the Notes,[13] but here are some of the highlights from their study and in their words:

Key points

- Compared to regular video and content, 360-degree video/VR received higher engagement. This can be measured by the number of video completions, clicks and overall engagement rate.

- Brands using 360-degree videos/VR are spread across all verticals. Content quality in this industry has dramatically improved every year. And distribution is a critical part to determine campaign success.

- Different distribution channels require different metrics and KPIs that need to be measured. We have found a way to measure these metrics across all channels. For ads, you can leverage existing third-party ad validation to verify the performance.

Other markets using VR

Outside of the marketing industry, we are seeing huge growth in the use of VR for health care, design, training and education. Let's take a quick look at some of these industries and how they are using VR.

Health care

Virtual reality is set to radically disrupt the health-care sector. In 2017, Professor Shafi Ahmed, 'the VR Doctor' and founder of Medical Realities, used a mixed-reality headset (Microsoft Hololens) to first plan an operation with specialists in Mumbai and London and then to aid communication internationally during the actual operation, live.[14] This allowed some of the world's best specialists in this particular kind of operation to be virtually present at the same moment and share knowledge. In 2016 Professor Ahmed had also live streamed in 360 during open heart surgery, allowing trainee doctors anywhere in the world to watch.[15] The ability to operate or collaborate virtually in health care is just the tip of a huge iceberg of potential for VR to revolutionize health care.

In the operating theatre, surgeons are able to train, performing virtual operations where they even have force feedback called 'haptics', allowing them to understand that they have hit bone or are moving through softer tissue. They are able to take scans of patients pre-operation and then move inside the body, via the scan, and understand the unique issues that each case is about to throw at them – before they even lift a scalpel. The parallel development with robotics will allow for virtual surgeries that use far more precision and dexterity than the human hand could ever achieve.

VR for health care goes far beyond the operating theatre, with significant research being conducted into depression, anxiety, post-traumatic stress disorder (PTSD) and many more physiological applications. One particularly interesting study by University College London (UCL) and Catalan Institution for Research and Advanced Studies (ICREA) in 2017 allows patients with depression to enter a room in VR and try to calm a crying child in the corner.[16] Their resulting efforts are fully captured from a full motion capture suit, allowing them to revisit the room, later in the week, and experience the same thing but from the perspective of the child. They are being soothed and calmed by a virtual version of themselves. For PTSD, technicians work with patients to try to re-create the moments that led to the stress. Amazingly, this kind of exposure is (counter-intuitively) one of the best forms of treatment.

'Big pharma' has been moving fast into VR too. One of the largest areas has been in disease awareness. Abbvie produced an experience that simulates what it is like to have Parkinson's disease, taking you through seemingly mundane real-life experiences such as shopping, and showing the complications and frustrations it brings.[17] One of the more innovative experiences was from GSK, who combined a VR headset with a pair of cameras, allowing you to see the world through the eyes of someone having a migraine, a truly frightening and eye-opening experience.[18] Other experiences have focused on empathizing with people with autism and epilepsy (the latter being one of ours).

Rehabilitation and physiotherapy also look to benefit hugely from VR. One of the most difficult parts of any recovery, be it from a stroke or a car crash, is the application of and sticking to a routine of laborious (and often very uncomfortable) exercises. What if you could make these exercises fun though, put on a headset and be in a game environment where doing your exercises earns you points! Where you can see that the ark in which you are moving your arm during a stretch is misaligned with the perfect movement that was recorded with your doctor. Your doctor could remotely monitor your progress, being alerted if your participation falls below a certain level or if your score is regularly poor. You are saved in regular visits, the doctor can monitor you more efficiently and your recovery is greatly sped up.

We are seeing huge innovation and application of VR in health care; on the surface it is at trade shows and in the press with early applications in hospitals, but under the surface a whole industry is being developed that is going to drastically transform patient treatment, disease awareness, diagnosis and marketing.

Design

Virtual reality allows architects, automotive designers, product designers and more to truly visualize their designs. One of the most beneficial aspects of VR in design is its ability to put you inside the design on a 1:1 scale. This means an architect does not need to rely on example sketches or cardboard modelling but can actually walk inside their structures. They can show clients literally how the building is going to look rather than leaving it to the imagination.

Nearly all automotive marques are using VR in some part in the design process. London design agency Seymourpowell has built a platform for collaborative car design using the HTC Vive. Multiple people can work together on a design from any part of the world.[19] Gravity Sketch, the stunning, VR-enabled 3D design tool, is also being heavily used by the automotive industry.[20] It allows designers to quickly build a life-size 3D model and then import it into more traditional 3D modelling platforms, essentially freeing up the most creative part of the process to be done with the most natural movements possible.

Training

The training sector is another big growth area for VR – simply put, a virtual version of staff training can reduce the need for travel, reduce the need for physical resources, reduce health and safety risks for hazardous training and be more engaging and more trackable than conventional training. In short, the training industry is starting to benefit massively from VR.

One of the best uses of VR in staff training is to create realistic scenarios specific to the role. By being able to control this virtual world, companies can formulate all types of experiences that may not have been possible otherwise. These incidents can be tailored to replicate any potential business crises so that employers can also analyse users' stress levels and problem-solving skills. We completed a project for Deloitte in 2015 that allowed them to simulate a series of breaches of data security and client confidentiality. From the perspective of a staff member you had to spot these breaches in other staff and then choose what to do in response.

Typically Deloitte would do their training using videos – sitting staff in rooms with TVs and showing the training videos, then testing them on paper/computer questionnaires. Using the VR app, the subjects feel like they are there, in the scenario: people talk to them in the scene and they have to make decisions based on the 'real' world around them. This is far more engaging, plus, has the added bonus of being able to let Deloitte know people's scores, reaction times and any other data you could require.

When it comes to more hazardous training, Walmart has equipped 200 of its academies with a VR training programme that immerses employees in challenging circumstances such as spills or holiday rushes.[21] In the words of Walmart, 'From our test, we've seen that associates who go through VR training retain what they have learnt in those situations better than those who haven't.'

Education

VR is a captivating way to learn, being virtually transported to the moon for the first landing, or to the time of the dinosaurs or other historical moments will be commonplace for the schools of the future. Field trips to local farms will be replaced with virtual safaris and the 'big five' being at touching distance.

Google Expeditions was one of the first attempts at using VR for education – for the cost of a cardboard (literally) headset, children could be transported to coral reefs, the surface of Mars, Aztec temples and much more.[22] By June 2017 Google had reached over 2 million students and is now branching out into augmented reality education too. There is a fascinating podcast, interviewing Jennifer Holland, Google Daydream's Education Programme Manager, on Voices of VR.[23]

Education does not have to be for children though, but it can be for adults too – causal learning. Or it can be part of exhibitions in museums. Take the Science Museum in London, which has two VR experiences, first was the Handley Page experience, and second, the Tim Peak Space Descent. The Handley Page experience allows you to see a virtual version of one of the earliest aircraft (built in 1928) and to learn about how its ground-breaking aerodynamics allowed it to fly.[24]

Conclusion

We can see there are a number of reasons that VR is a powerful medium for a brand or business to connect with customers. You can show a real place, product or service with great authenticity, transporting viewers into the heart of your brand. You can connect with customers on a more intense and emotional level than other mediums allow, a case in point being the explosion of 'empathy VR' for charities.

Our project KPIs, anecdotal evidence from other VR studios and split tests done by Google point to huge successes from well-thought-through projects. Given the number of headsets in the market though, a campaign must be carefully thought through to target people either with physical activations (bringing the tech to them) or with cheaper headset giveaways such as branded Google Cardboards.

VR also enables brands and businesses to 'wow' their customers – the majority of people still have not tried VR and it is an incredibly intense and high-impact medium. People will talk about and remember your brand after a well-thought-out VR experience. This novel effect of first VR use is fast wearing off though and experiences are more and more judged on their merit rather than novelty, so strike fast if you still want that inherent first-time-user bonus!

Notes

1 BirdLife International (2017) [accessed 8 April 2018] *Walk With Penguins* [Online] https://www.birdlife.org/worldwide/news/walk-penguins-ground-breaking-virtual-reality-video & http://visualise.com/case-study/walk-with-penguins

2 Médecins Sans Frontières (Doctors Without Borders) (2017) [accessed 8 April 2018] Forced from home [Online] http://www.forcedfromhome.com/360-videos/ & http://visualise.com/case-study/msf-doctors-without-borders-forced-home

3 The Void [accessed 8 April 2018] Star Wars – Secrets of the Empire VR Experience [Online] https://www.thevoid.com/dimensions/starwars/secretsoftheempire/

4 Visualise (2016) [accessed 8 April 2018] Try Before You Fly – Thomas Cook [Online] http://visualise.com/case-study/thomas-cook-virtual-holiday

5 Lowe's 'Holorooms' [accessed 8 April 2018] Information on the Lowes VR experiences [Online] http://www.lowesinnovationlabs.com/holoroom/

6 App Store [accessed 8 April 2018] Ikea place app on Apple iOS [Online] https://itunes.apple.com/gb/app/ikea-place/id1279244498?mt=8

7 YouTube [accessed 8 April 2018] Waitrose Tuna 360, adam&eveDDB, Outsider and Visualise (2017) [Online] http://www.adamandeveddb.com/work/project/tuna and https://www.youtube.com/watch?v=Fb5qqQPOLeM

8 Visualise (2015) [accessed 8 April 2018] British Army VR Experience, Visualise [Online] http://visualise.com/case-study/british-army-vr-recruitment-experience

9 *Financial Times* (2016) [accessed 8 April 2018] Hidden Cities Rio, Google and Visualise [Online] https://hiddencities.ft.com/rio

10 Within, Clouds Over Sidra (2015) [accessed 8 April 2018] [Online] https://with.in/watch/clouds-over-sidra/

11 The Sidra Project (2015) [accessed 8 April 2018] Clouds Over Sidra [Online] http://thesidraproject.ca/about/

12 Habig, J [accessed 8 April 2018] Think with Google, is 360 video worth it? (July 2016) [Online] https://www.thinkwithgoogle.com/advertising-channels/video/360-video-advertising/

13 Phaisan, B [accessed 8 April 2018] Omnivirt, 360° video/VR performance statistics from 1000+ campaigns (13 November 2017)

[Online] https://www.omnivirt.com/blog/360-video-vr-performance-statistics/

14 Lay, K [accessed 8 April 2018] VR surgeons put headsets together in a global first, *The Times* (24 October 2017) [Online] https://www.thetimes.co.uk/article/vr-surgeons-put-headsets-together-in-a-global-first-hmz9g6bt6

15 Volpicelli, G [accessed 8 April 2018] What's next for VR surgery? *Wired* (14 April 2016) [Online] http://www.wired.co.uk/article/wired-health-virtual-reality-surgery-shafi-ahmed

16 Dayantis, H [accessed 8 April 2018] Virtual reality therapy could help people with depression, *UCL News* (15 February 2016) [Online] http://www.ucl.ac.uk/news/news-articles/0216/150216-virtual-reality-treat-depression

17 The Virtual Dutchmen (2016) [accessed 8 April 2018] VR Parkinson's experience [Online] https://www.youtube.com/watch?v=t0a1ggZH4Bk

18 GSK (2016) [accessed 8 April 2018] The Excedrin® migraine experience [Online] https://www.youtube.com/watch?v=tco5QMTfxKM

19 Seymourpowell (2017) [accessed 8 April 2018] Automotive design tool [Online] https://www.youtube.com/watch?time_continue=87&v=-4PTdB9dnsw

20 Gravity Sketch (2018) [accessed 8 April 2018] [Online] https://www.gravitysketch.com/vr/

21 Harris, B (31 May 2017) [accessed 8 April 2018] Walmart VR training [Online] https://blog.walmart.com/opportunity/20170531/from-football-to-retail-virtual-reality-debuts-in-associate-training

22 Google Expeditions Project (2017) [accessed 8 April 2018] [Online] https://edu.google.com/expeditions/#about

23 Voices of VR Podcast (27 May 2017) [accessed 8 April 2018] #539: Google Expeditions is leading innovation in the future of immersive education, feat Jennifer Holland [Online] http://voicesofvr.com/539-google-expeditions-is-leading-innovation-in-the-future-of-immersive-education/

24 Science Museum (2 November 2016) [accessed 8 April 2018] The Science Museum and Samsung to bring exciting digital enhancements to new mathematics gallery [Online] https://www.sciencemuseum.org.uk/about-us/press-office/science-museum-and-samsung-bring-exciting-digital-enhancements-new

Industry insights

02

Interviews with the best
in the VR business

In this chapter I interview some of the leading figures in the VR industry. People who have either created or overseen the production of campaigns that have been hugely successful for their clients. Their insight is vital in understanding the thinking behind VR campaigns to date. Although I started out with the same broad set of questions, often the conversation moved in unexpected directions, revealing aspects of VR marketing that I had not thought about.

In order to understand the industry, these experts will explain key examples they were involved with and their thoughts on marketing in VR more generally. The people interviewed range from managing partners in creative agencies, creative directors, innovation specialists and even just futurists with a good overview of the industry as a whole.

First though, I was lucky enough to talk to SuperData, who have shared some of their latest sets of numbers from headset sales and usage, a good foundation to understand before we read the following interviews.

Virtual reality industry health

Stephanie Llamas, VP, Research and Strategy, Head of Immersive Technology Insights: SuperData Research

INTERVIEW

Stuart: So how do you see the current health of the VR industry?

Llamas: We started out thinking that, this year, we would see a few more monetization opportunities for consumer products than we did. We are finding that on the Steam side of course there are upfront purchases, so you can purchase a whole game at once. But other than that we are seeing that there is a hard time for other segments to break into revenue streams for VR.

Part of the revenue stall is more a result of that than quality content. I think there is plenty of quality content but part of the problem also is that if the studios cannot make money then they cannot keep creating.

You mentioned in your e-mail, this shift to Enterprise, and that has a lot to do with it. There is a much clearer monetization path there. We knew that Enterprise had a lot of revenue opportunity compared to consumer, but I think just part of it was the expectation that more consumers would be willing to spend and that more of these platforms had an idea of how they would spend.

The other thing obviously is adoption, although our adoption numbers certainly are smaller than they were at the beginning of the year. I still think this was a good year for adoption considering the requirements you need for the supporting hardware. For Oculus and Vive they really both were able to also capture a secondary market, not just the first adopters but people who were kind of curious and maybe were just getting on board with higher-end PCs or seeing an opportunity to get good deals on this hardware versus last year. So I'm actually fairly impressed that Oculus and Vive were able to sustain themselves with these positive shipment numbers. Also PlayStation, just the sheer penetration of PS4 globally is over 70 million right now and does really help their ability to increase adoption on the PSVR side. I think that has given them a lot more confidence when it comes to marketing and supply. But the adoption rate compared to the number of PS4s out there is still a little low.

Sony has promised a lot of really compelling content for next year. If that's the case, if they are able to bring on more and more popular intellectual property (IP), like they have with Skyrim and Fallout and those more popular games such as Resident Evil, then there is certainly an opportunity to gain more market share. There is disappointment with the VR industry and therefore slow growth; they kind of work in tandem, so slow growth and less investment and adoption brings expectations down, which also brings confidence down, so then consumers are adopting less, and so on. But just with the opportunities that we're seeing in enterprise, I think there is going to be a lot more growth for companies to be able to fund themselves through business applications and use that to fuel their consumer-facing content.

Stuart: How do you think headset sales at the premium end performed?

Llamas: I think Oculus did a good job in finding a price point that secondary adopters would be more comfortable with. When first adopters did their research, at the time Oculus didn't have true room scale, they didn't have the touch yet, etc. So if you were going to go all in on VR you were going to go for the Vive. Spend a little extra money but get a much fuller experience. But now that Oculus has that added functionality they have done a fairly good job of finding a price point that helps move the product. I think the main challenge is still educating the consumer in terms of set-up – it is still not completely straightforward what is needed. If you're talking about our first adopter audience then they are going to look into how many sensors they need, what does the bundle come with, and so on.

Stuart: What do you think about the Oculus Go? Will that have a big effect on the market?

Llamas: I think it depends. It could if it's high-enough quality and if it's something that is impressive to general consumers. It could have a fairly big impact because the biggest hurdle right now for adoption is friction, and adoption comes from education and affordability.

So untethering is one part of that – the support of hardware needed, the set-up for it. Windows has done a much better job than Vive and Oculus right now, in terms of making it seamless. Set-up and getting into an experience is fairly easy, there is less friction. I wouldn't say Oculus or Vive are particularly hard to set up, but you do have to deal with things like the sensors. Even just turning it on and getting started when you first open the box – it is much easier with Windows headsets. That kind of frictionless experience is what is really needed. Even then, though, Windows got in too late and early adopters already had their Oculus and Vive, and general consumers were not going to get on board. If Oculus Go is able to give consumers seamlessness along with untethering, in a way that not even mobile devices have been able to do, then I think that is going to have a really positive impact on adoption. But a $200 device, I don't know what the quality is going to be – $200 is a better price point, but if you are trying to access an audience that is not as enthusiastic about VR as the people who are on it now, they are still going to be fairly critical at that price point.

You have the people who are very enthusiastic about VR and therefore are going to spend on a higher-value experience, and then you have people for who $200 is still not worth the perceived novelty.

Stuart: What are some of the highlights from your research?

Llamas: On the consumer side, one thing that has been particularly interesting is location-based VR and the potential for that. You have arcades that have shown mixed success. But there is a lot of really promising content that we think is going to be the spark for VR awareness. As you start to see more experiences like the Void's Ghostbusters or Jumanji, or things like that, where people recognize the IP and are already excited about it, and then get this opportunity to do something that they would not otherwise be able to do – especially people who are not consumers of VR right now.

Stuart: So are you talking about 'VRcades'?

Llamas: VRcades and location-based experiences like The Void, experiences that have been moving around the country (United States), and some other interesting activations from brands. Public spaces, like malls, where people don't exactly know what VR is and wouldn't otherwise have the opportunity to try it are really essential to driving awareness of the potential of VR. That's why I think Oculus Go could be really symbiotic to that. You could get people inside of these really interesting location-based experiences, which are so enticing to these consumers who would never have tried VR, and then they realize they could get involved for just $200.

They have to think about the turnover challenge though: getting enough people through at a price that makes a profit while providing a full-enough experience to justify the spend. I think also incorporating those experiences into theme parks will be big. One thing theme parks have always been really good at is adopting these really interesting experiences and technologies, like 3D and 4D where people try the medium for the first time. People may come for the other rides, but they will try VR/AR there.

Stuart: What other areas do you see VR growing in?

Llamas: In the workplace, VR training and simulations can produce a more educated, safer workforce. This is where we are seeing the biggest interest in enterprise. What is going to be most interesting is seeing how that affects efficiency and economies on a larger scale while bringing attention to MR, AR and VR to different sectors, from governments to companies that are not even really thinking about it or what it is. So it is going to have a much larger-scale effect on society as a whole, which will show how transformative it actually is.

Virtual reality in tourism

South Africa Tourism VR project: Andy Corcoran, Managing Partner Creative Services, Head of UM Studios

One of the first VR projects in Europe – Corcoran's idea. Shot in 2013, the South Africa Tourism (SAT) VR project took you to some of the highlights of the country – face to face with elephants, abseiling down Table Mountain, shark diving, into the hipster heart of Johannesburg and much more. Crucially it was also one of the first projects to use both 360 visuals and 360 audio. Visualise produced the VR video content and the content agency Somethin' Else built the binaural engine.

INTERVIEW

Stuart: Why did you want to use VR for this campaign?

Corcoran: South Africa Tourism wanted to do something different, to draw attention from the likes of Canada and Australia. They wanted to use a medium that allowed them to transport people to the heart of a country and experiences that people may on the surface be resistant to – for example, markets in the heart of Johannesburg. They had to use a medium that broke through people's preconceived ideas.

At the time, doing anything different in the tourism sector meant the client was already winning. However, the main reason was to allow people to form new opinions, and dispel preconceptions.

This kind of first-mover advantage for companies experimenting with VR was too often the only reason VR was produced. The beauty of the SAT project was that it was just part of the reasoning.

INTERVIEW

Corcoran: Immersing someone in parts of South Africa that show the country's vibrant culture, potential for adventure tourism and unrivalled beauty allowed people to see for themselves what a holiday to South Africa could be like and dispel any myths they may have had. Crucially they felt they were putting the clients 'into' South Africa, in a way that allowed them to make their own decisions about it. They were not *telling* them, just opening a door and saying 'see for yourself'.

Stuart: Were there any difficulties in using VR for this campaign?

Corcoran: We knew straight away that we needed to find a clever way to bring this content to people – there were not the headsets out there that there are now, so a series of events was decided upon. You are asking someone to do quite a lot actually – to trust an advertiser, not only say yes to a commercial message: I'm also going to put some crazy glasses on and watch a video to the end. These events invited travel and trade press to South African-themed evenings with drinks and entertainment, with the highlight being these beautifully designed pods, with tribal curtains keeping them private and high-end Oculus headsets and headphones perched by a stool.

But the campaign really took off from a completely unexpected direction – Facebook 360 Video. That's where things really went crazy. Soon after Facebook announced their compatibility, the video was chopped up into different parts and uploaded to the new 360 platform. In a week we got 5 million views of the content, which was beyond our wildest dreams.

Stuart: Is VR a valuable form of marketing?

Corcoran: 360 videos on YouTube and Facebook are a game changer but of course not nearly as immersive as having a headset on. With well-built VR experiences you can create advocates – people who talk about your client/product, people who are emotionally engaged. These may just be 5 per cent of the people you are reaching out to but those people will go on to convert others. So you are creating richer and deeper experiences, featuring rewarding content that is going to chime with these people. VR is perfect for that.

Stuart: Do you think VR is ready now, or is it too early? Is it a fad?

Corcoran: Look at the content that is popping, it's handheld, it's unedited, it's authentic. It's UGC [user-generated content]. VR is not – in 2017 it's specially produced, on similar budgets and quality standards to TV or commercial production, it's high production values. If you know that all this rough-and-ready, spontaneous, user-generated content or talent-led video is exploding, how do we get that in VR...

I think this is a brilliant point by Andy, as 360 video gets more accessible to the masses and the quality of consumer cameras increases, as it already is at a startling pace. We are going to start getting more and more established influencers using the medium to pull people into their worlds, and of course, where this happens, marketers will follow.

INTERVIEW

Corcoran: As you know I'm a technophile, I take my Ricoh Theta S on holiday with me, wander down to the beach with it, get to show my mates and parents where I've been. But a camera like that, it's been out for a few years now and it's still £300, that's too high.

Andy's angle here is particularly interesting when you contrast it to how a lot of people answer this question – they look at headset quality and development and content for those headsets but not at user-generated content driving the market from the bottom up – with consumer 360 video cameras.

INTERVIEW

Corcoran: We work through the whole year as an agency with bloggers, influencers, talent – we have a whole area of the business dedicated to this and managing those relationships. As soon as they have something they can do that brings their regular world to life, of which there are 3 million subscribers or whatever that is, suddenly, you've got this super-premium version of communication from that person – an experience involving the person you love to follow, rather than a standard video or article – then everyone will want to watch that.

Stuart: What problems do you think VR solves?

Corcoran: If you go to see DCM [Digital Cinema Media – a company involved in advertising during the trailers of films], they talk about a captive audience and what that attention is worth, brand recall, etc, and in cinemas it is through the roof. It is also because it's a special occasion visiting the cinema, it's known as a 'lean forward medium', where you have paid premium ticket prices to watch something you are excited about – as such, you are all eyes and ears. They have stats around brand recall and heightened emotional response that show that the same ad on TV and the cinema will be far more successful in the cinema. It is the same argument that you can make for VR.

This captive audience and heightened emotional state that VR can bring does mean, though, that you have to be responsible. The content has to be less conspicuously an advert, less obviously a sell, and brands need to think about how they can credibly entertain their audience, because if they can't then it won't work in VR. It's a brand promise you can't break.

Brands need to use VR responsibly so as to not turn people off the medium with overly advertorial content and experiences that jar or are dull.

Stuart: Are there any examples of VR you want to mention?

Corcoran: As a freebie for *Spider-Man: Homecoming* on PSVR, they launched a short game to coincide with the film launch. As the VR audience is not a mass audience you can treat them differently, that's what Marvel did. The experience is really fun and gets you talking – when your friends are over you show them, they talk… etc.

This last point by Corcoran really got me thinking. You get a chance to be Spider-Man, who wouldn't want to do that? Isn't that what half the Marvel films are about – ordinary people who get extraordinary abilities? Here is a medium that let's you be that hero – VR allows that! As the technology and experiences get better, it will feel more and more real and you will be able to live out your Marvel fantasies in (virtual) reality. If that's not a route to mass adoption then I don't know what is!

Virtual reality in entertainment and sport

Richard Nockles – Founder of Surround Vision and VR Creative Director at Sky

Richard started out his career by setting up the UK arm of 360 video content creation company Yellow Bird in 2011 and, as such, was one of the pioneers in 360 content production in Europe.

INTERVIEW

Stuart: You have been in this industry for longer than anyone else I know, how did you start?

Nockles: I discovered 360 through Immersive Media, run then by Myles McGovern, who is an absolute legend of the industry. The first time I got involved was when I saw one of their dodeca camera systems, which had been put in Miami stadium – you could click with your mouse and look around the stadium.

Interestingly, as a bit of history as well, Google commissioned Immersive Media to capture 35 cities with this camera as the beginning of street view. This was the initial design of the street view camera!

I contacted anyone I could who had one of these cameras and tried to hire them out. The dodeca cameras were incredibly difficult to rent, and when you could find them you were paying around £6,000 per day to use them – hard to justify for playing around with.

The only other alternative was the Ladybug Camera, a company called Yellow Bird in Holland happened to have one so I started talking to them. With my background in '360 Digital', not to be confused with 360 immersive, I had an understanding of interactive clickable hotspots, marketing, work with brands on 'lean forward' digital concepts, etc – it was a perfect fit.

Early work with the cameras was difficult, the cameras were unreliable but we still managed to get some amazing footage. We did the first-ever 360 live project with the BBC and Blue Peter, work with ITV and Channel 4. In fact, the most successful project to date for me, still, in terms of the marketing value, engagement time and metrics, was the Channel 4 project we did with Damien Hirst.

Damien Hirst Gallery 360 (2012)

INTERVIEW

Nockles: The piece involved a series of pieces, moving round his exhibition at the Tate Modern, London. Noel Fielding was the presenter and at the peak of his popularity. Damien Hirst could be seen sitting in the background of some of the shots. The average time spent on the experience was 18 minutes and we had 120,000 online views of the video.

This was pre-recorded and then delivered on to the UK TV Channel 4 website and app. The project worked in HTML5, which meant access crucially to mobile. Now the reason the average time was 18 minutes was because we had a lot of added interactivity in the scene – clickable video, launching 16×9 interviews with the show curators. It was a really amazing piece of content for art lovers; there was a dedicated fan base for both Damien Hirst and for the Tate. Finally, having Noel Fielding brought in a whole different demographic.

Since then I'm still banging that same drum – close proximity, presenter led, engaging and intimate.

I think it is interesting how techniques developed for shooting 360 on the 'flat screen' deliverables of desktop and mobile are still so relevant today on VR headsets. From a technical aspect, the reason for that must be that we have the same ultimate restrictions in lens types, sensor quality and pixelation of displays. From a creative perspective the issue of how best to guide the viewer remains – no better way of doing that than a charismatic presenter like Noel Fielding.

INTERVIEW

Stuart: Tell me more about your role at Sky.

Nockles: Sky really understands VR and its future potential. That is why, as a broadcaster, Sky is investing in a team called Sky VR Studios. It is an innovation hub, a chance for them to play and experiment before VR fully kicks off. Sky sees the future of broadcast delivery as being in a real-time engine, in fact, a lot of Sky's current programming already uses them. Platforms like Unity (typically known for building computer games) are being used now to place 3D graphics and information over live TV.

So Sky is getting great PR from its work in VR but is also experimenting with a technology that works in parallel with its current development models towards real-time engine-assisted TV.

The department at Sky VR studios is run by inspired technical artists who, by pushing the boundaries, are in turn influencing other departments with their developments through osmosis. There is a can-do culture at Sky. It's rare. I'm told no, I can't do that – Sky always wants to try something new.

Stuart: Is Sky partnering with any brands with its VR?

Nockles: The use of VR for marketing is a really interesting spot for Sky, because very often there will be perfect partners in brands that can come up with something that is very sharable and sticky, benefiting both them and the broadcaster. Sky is looking to combine the platform (Sky VR) with the brand (eg Nike) and the talent (eg Wayne Rooney) to create content that drives engagement and an increase in the number of users.

Stuart: Do you think that VR is a valuable form of marketing?

Nockles: Yes, when it is used for the right reason. As with other mediums, you need to understand your audience, who you want to reach, what kind of budget you have, etc. VR still pierces through the noise, journalists still favour these projects. It still is exciting and talked about. If you do something like Surround Vision does, or Visualise or Rewind, that is educated, informed, done well – then yes it is of value.

Stuart: What is the appeal of VR outside of PR for a brand?

Nockles: Engagement, put a headset on someone and you have their full attention. The issue is guaranteeing you can get it on their heads though! Sure you can have a 'magic window' [the industry term for viewing a 360 video on a mobile phone or tablet, where the device displays the content like you are looking through a window into another world] but the effect of this only lasts around 15 seconds before people put it down. It does not have the same impact as a headset.

Stuart: What are the main issues of VR?

Nockles: I think the human race is inherently social and that isolating ourselves in headsets is quite frightening. So the likes of mixed reality and applications in VR that allow you to enjoy experiences with your friends are key.

Nockles: At Surround Vision, we are developing live volumetric capture, so you can watch games and events with your friends in a very natural way. Why restrict yourself to the sidelines when you can wander the pitch and walk up to the net. If you can capture volumetric in real time – well, that's the end game.

Stuart: Do you think VR is a fad?

Nockles: I think it is 100 per cent the future, it will just take a little while to take off. We're 10 years away from where it will get to – being a fully usable, social world. You will be able to pay to go to matches, watch them with your friends in a row and watch from the best seats in the house, whilst all being in different physical locations.

When I have grandchildren they are going to be laughing at the fact that I used to open up a laptop – with future interfaces in the virtual world we just cannot even imagine how good it is going to be.

VR ultimately will be a way of transporting people seamlessly to incredible events and places to experience life and imagine life like nothing else.

Stuart: What advice would you give to a brand approaching VR?

Nockles: The same rules apply to other mediums – you have to capture people's attention. There are far too many pieces around that are too slow to move and lose people right at the start. You need to engage, be playful, be energetic, be social and try something different.

Stuart: What is the best example of VR you have seen for marketing?

Nockles: Funnily enough, a project that was aimed at 100 people, the heads of state for the Paris Climate Change Accord. The project was a 360 video that tells the story of an ambitious plan to build a great green wall across Africa in combat with desertification.

All of the key heads of state watched this in headset – Merkel, Cameron, sadly not Obama but a host of others and as a result they committed US $4 billion to this campaign.

Stuart: How do you think VR will evolve?

Nockles: I think that VR's future is in real time – I don't like to say game engines as it seems to put people off, but real-time engines. The way we produce content now – 360 video will be irrelevant in the future. Unless of course it's an exceptional moment, then it will always have a value, but the tech and techniques for production will be totally different. We will be looking at volumetric capture that allows the director to actually choose viewpoints or guide the viewer after they have actually done the capture!

The technologist's view

Andy Hood, Head of Emerging Technologies at AKQA

Andy has been at AKQA since 1999 and is one of the most respected industry experts in new technologies and their applications for brands.

INTERVIEW

Stuart: Can you explain your role at AKQA?

Hood: The emerging technologies role is something created four/five years ago when I realized that the way to enable people to innovate is for people to understand: not what things do and how they work but what they actually mean. So it is highlighting the problems that things can solve or they create, but more importantly the behaviours that either they change or that need to change in order for them to be adopted. Finally, it is to understand how these changing behaviours will shape the world.

Nissan IDx experience

INTERVIEW

Stuart: Can you tell us about your Nissan IDx experience?

Hood: At the Tokyo motor show, Nissan was launching two new concept cars. These concept cars were designed to be co-created with Nissan when you bought them. Not just configuration – I'll have the spoiler and leopard-skin interior, etc – but more to do with matching the car to your personality and character. We were looking at what you could think of as slightly more orthodox ways to launch the car – big screens, gesture, etc – but then Oculus emerged from Kickstarter, having funded it some time ago we had our headset arrive half-way through this project. We tried it out, and realized that it could be used for this project.

We realized at that point that thrills, adrenaline, excitement and screaming was not what we were selling... We were going to sell access – virtual reality gives you access to objects and places that you don't have access to because they are too far away, you cannot afford them, because they don't exist yet or because the laws of physics prevent it happening. We came to that conclusion in a matter of hours.

Actually it is the presence of the objects in the room and your feeling of direct access to them that is the selling point of VR to anyone outside the gaming community. Having done that we realized that what Nissan needed – in launching two concept cars that did not actually exist yet – was to provide people with the direct access they craved to those vehicles. Virtual reality also allowed for the process of co-creation, which would have been impossible with a physical unit standing in front of you.

We created journeys that you could venture through, where you made choices about your lifestyle that were then reflected in the engineering choices on the car. So you moved through scene to scene and there were lots of different ways the scenes could play out. There was a cool-looking robotic samurai and a sleek-looking cyber ninja and you would choose between them – the ninja representing quiet, conservation of energy, electric engine and the samurai representing a more overt display of power.

We had a foreground hero object, the car, that we wanted to focus on, but you also have journeys and scenery that you want people to engage with. There is therefore a balance needed between exploration of the environment you are in, journeying through the scenes/scenarios, and focus and interrogation of the hero object. The balance between these three things is vital from a user-experience point of view.

It wasn't a demo but a fully fleshed-out experience. In terms of the problems new technologies solve and the behavioural changes needed, generally there is a period of time needed to work these things out. You come to conclusions gradually through using the tech and talking to people and then you formalize and codify this knowledge and this becomes what you run with. In this case we had to do that instantly.

At this point Hood makes an aside about 360 video:

INTERVIEW

Hood: The interesting thing to us, that we put to use with Nissan, was the total fixation on the need for interaction. True immersion does not happen without interaction. So much that people think is VR, or call VR, is actually just 360.

At the Cannes Lions Festival in France, I was president at the mobile jury; there was a 360 video category and a VR category and some things were in both. Nothing in the VR category was shortlisted, not one thing. Some things in the 360 category ended up getting silvers and golds. Simply having a 360 video that you can watch in a headset does not make something virtual reality. It is just another way to view a 360 video.

This is a fascinating example of the argument in the industry about 360 video – Andy Hood is right, technically, from a definition perspective. However, I posit to him later that 360 video is a very valid format on headsets whether it is labelled as VR or not.

Back to Nissan:

INTERVIEW

Hood: In order to allow for interaction we had to look at the method. At the time you had game controllers, but these took you out of the experience, so the next idea was to replicate 'eye tracking' although really it was head movement tracking. The idea that you look at something to trigger an interaction, move through a scene, make decisions about things, etc. This was trying to allow you to do with your head what the kinect on the X-Box would let you do with your hands. This has become a standard technique now in VR, at the time, though, we had to work it out.

We also created a headset, using the Oculus Rift, that you had to hold like a pair of binoculars. This meant that you moved your head in a natural way. We found that when people were fully strapped into an unmodified Oculus they were not moving their head much. Things that we worked out for Nissan came together really well.

Another thing we realized with Nissan was that the fixation with things needing to be photo real was a red herring. Immersion is not obtained through the reality of the environment, but through the authenticity of the experience you have. So you could have a really abstract experience but you can be fully immersed in it if the feeling you have is authentic. A beautiful, photo-realized environment that does not feel or react quite right can leave you feeling detached.

The issue of CG assets looking nearly real and therefore worse than something more abstract is a familiar issue to the film world. With regards to human 'photorealism' the roboticist Masahiro Mori coined the phrase 'uncanny valley' to describe the issue whereby nearly real-looking robots were viewed with repulsion and fear whereas 100 per cent perfect-looking or completely unreal-looking humanoids were not.

INTERVIEW

Hood: We only had eight weeks to do this, from start to finish, having never done it, opening Unity for the first time with some of our developers.

Stuart: Were there any key performance indicators (KPIs) or metrics from the project?

Hood: There were interesting KPIs that emerged from the project but less going into it. In that period, installations tended not to have a lot of hard metrics around them. However, post event, the data generated was very interesting. We stored all the configurations and choices people had made in different parts of the world. We had numbers of people who had chosen different routes, configurations, journeys and were able to compare these between the locations of Japan, the UK and the United States. There were very different trends in the different countries.

Were this experience to have been extended and the data analysed over a longer period then it would have been very revealing and no doubt could have informed car development.

Stuart: At the end of the experience, was there any way of sharing it?

Hood: We generated images of your specific version of the car that could be shared after you had completed the experience at the show.

Stuart: Was the client happy with the project? Did they see it as a success?

Hood: Yes, very much so – their stand was the 'must-see' experience of the show, with people queuing for over an hour for their turn. It was repeated in Detroit, and then at Goodwood, with excellent results. These were the early days of the modern era of VR, using the pre-Facebook Oculus Rift, so both we and our clients were happy to use this medium to great effect.

Stuart: What was the reason to use VR, from Nissan's perspective?

Hood: When we showed them the roller-coaster, so they could understand immersion in VR, then showed them a simple app we had built with a car in a white room, which could have components changed on it, it was the explanation we gave them around presence, access and immersion that was the reason they did it. This was pre all the main hype around Oculus; they did not even know that this technology was available when we brought it to them.

Had we brought this project to them six months later then I think the excitement around the fact that they could associate themselves with VR would have been a big driver.

Stuart: Do you find it harder to sell VR to brands now that it has gone beyond its peak hype?

Hood: Yes, it is difficult while VR is the biggest part of the conversation. I would never go to a client and say let's talk about virtual reality and explore what it can do for you. I would never do that. I would work out what problems the VR can solve, find clients with those problems, say to them 'You have this problem and we can solve it.' The fact that you are going to use VR only becomes apparent when they ask 'How are you going to solve it?' You have to have a problem and solution first, then you know you are using the VR authentically, to solve a problem. Rather than trying to retrofit a problem because you want to do VR.

When a client actually comes to see us and says 'let's talk about VR', my first thought is, are you coming to talk to us about VR because you know it is a solution to a problem you are going to talk to us about – or because you are just really excited about VR and want to do something with it?

Stuart: How can brands produce true VR/interactive VR experiences effectively, given there are so few headsets in the market?

Hood: Well this is the problem. Really there are two tiers of VR and they often get lumped together – high-end VR; Oculus Rift, HTC Vive, even PlayStation VR – these fully interactive, fully immersive platforms vs mobile VR. Perhaps excepting Samsung GearVR or Daydream, which sit between the two. But look at Google Cardboard. This is the ultimate way to view VR if you can get people to see it.

Cardboard did everyone a huge favour in allowing people to have access to a kind of pseudo-VR, entry level, taster course, without having to spend much money. Everyone has the hardware (phone); it's easy to distribute, companies brand it up. We did it with Martell. You can generate some reach using this.

It is easy to talk about Google Cardboard democratizing VR, but if you walked down the street and asked 100 people, I guarantee you would struggle to find one person who has even heard of it. So it is still very much in the bubble for the most part.

Cardboard has a very limited set of use cases because of the lack of interaction and lack of immersion. So you've got a lot of games, simple branded games, and 360 videos of views on beaches or first-person point-of-view (POV) experiences. There were some nicely realized versions of these but it is still relatively restricted.

The likes of Daydream and GearVR, though, show you how far mobile-based experiences can go. Take a look at *Fantastic Beasts*, for example. I think therefore that VR development got stuck for a couple of years with Cardboard with a genuine level of excitement but a barrier with the kind of experience you could create or the problems you could really solve. So there were a lot of pieces that were pure PR rather than having a utility value to them.

It is still a novelty to find someone with even a Daydream or GearVR. I was hoping that Samsung would launch the GearVR and then Apple would follow and then things would really kick off in a big way. People would want to be involved because it's Apple – regardless of what it is, they have that attachment. But Samsung doing it alone, with only their Galaxy phones compatible, is going to have a limited reach.

If you are talking to a client and you want to do something of value, the limited numbers of people who have headsets is always going to be a barrier. With clients there is always a tipping point where you say there are a certain number of people and they go for it. So if you look at say Amazon Echo, there is no way that the majority of people have got one. However, there is a large number of people with them, a high-enough number for clients to go down that route.

VR didn't get to that tipping point. Any number of headset figures we gave clients was not enough, they were excited about it but couldn't justify it.

The gap is between the utility of the experiences you can have with the devices you can get hold of versus the number of people who have got the devices that they need to have to do something special.

Stuart: What role do you think 360 video has played with VR?

Hood: Well it has kept the conversation alive, if it's 80 per cent of what you can do in a headset then it means that people are engaging with headsets still, while we wait for the technology to allow us to do what we need.

Stuart: Do you think that VR is a valuable form of marketing?

Hood: I think it can be, if it is done well and there are a few good examples, most of them in automotive. The reason why VR can be a really valuable marketing tool is because it doesn't just let you see the product but lets you have an authentic feel of the product. It can really change opinions, make something stick in the mind and be memorable, and even generate an emotional connection between a person and a brand.

If you give someone an amazing experience, and if they have achieved something, then you should let them share it. If you use it properly, if you get the data from it and create sharable assets and let people have agency, etc, then it is an incredibly powerful marketing tool.

If you imagine that the most incredible marketing tool of all would be to have people with you, person to person, in a controlled space that you own with your products doing what you want them to do with your product – you would teleport people into that. Well, you can't do that, but with VR you can get close and it is so much better than showing a video, playing them a song, showing some pictures.

Stuart: What advice would you give brands approaching VR for the first time?

Hood: I would say the main thing to do for a brand, investigating VR, is to spend the time actually learning about the medium and what it can do. What the value areas are. As a brand, if you are going to have a discussion with people you trust to bring about this value then it is useful to have a frame of reference. So they should do their homework, become informed, watch/play/interact with experiences out there. Get a range of VR headsets in the office, have industry experts come in and show them how it works. Go to VR conferences and listen to talks. Understand what your brand can get out of the medium. This is important for all mediums but particularly in VR, as such a new medium.

Stuart: If there is a metaverse how do you think marketing will work in there? How will marketing evolve in the virtual world?

Hood: You start thinking of virtual places where people meet up with each other and these places having almost traditional out-of-home advertising around them, which almost feels dystopian, what a shame that all that advertising follows us in there! There is a precedent for this though – just look at Fifa and all the marketing in there. It follows us everywhere we go.

I would like to think we could do better than that. Hopefully in the same way that there was a trend towards branded utility and branded content over straight images and messages advertising, this evolution will continue in VR. Brands sponsoring and attaching themselves to relevant features and services and offering a value they can be associated with would be a win-win. This would be much better than effectively having banners in the metaverse.

I suspect advertising will be much less overt in VR, at least I hope so. I think we will have more freedom of choice to escape these things – so the reason to interact with marketing will be because it provides you with value as a consumer.

Virtual reality in the automotive industry

Ross Wheeler, Head of Automotive and Board Director at Imagination

Ross Wheeler has been at Imagination since 1998 and now heads up their automotive team, overseeing clients such as Jaguar Land Rover, Rolls-Royce and Aston Martin globally. He oversaw one of the most successful and ambitious VR projects of the last few years – the VR launch of the Jaguar I-Pace.

Jaguar I-Pace VR launch

INTERVIEW

Stuart: Tell us about your work on the Jaguar I-Pace launch.

Wheeler: November 2016 at the LA auto show was the reveal of the new I-Pace. It is the all-electric concept for Jaguar, which is going to be their reply to Tesla. They came to us and asked what we could do with this car, how we could do something different – get into the right channels and get to the right people who are interested in this stuff.

We had already been doing some proofs of concepts in VR. Our tech team had been coming to me with ideas and examples of VR that I was not willing to put in front of the client, definitely not a luxury automotive player, because the quality of the VR was not good enough. They would just dismiss it outright.

One day, Russell Hall, our head tech sat me down and put the Vive on me, with a whole bunch of updates and said, 'Look at this.' I said 'Okay, this is something we can use. If not for full consumer contact but from the PR perspective of a car launch and reaching our specific targets.'

VR was at the very core of how this car had been designed – Jaguar Land Rover (JLR) had used VR to design their products anyway. So we thought we would do something with it.

We thought though, above the gimmicky side of VR, throwing snowballs or being on a roller-coaster, wouldn't it be great to do something bigger? What about making it truly social? So I set the challenge to the team: how do we bring everyone together? To get journalists, the automotive press, simultaneously in Germany, Los Angeles, London, wherever it might be but make them feel like they are all in the same room. Give them a virtual or even a real presenter, Ian Callum (the designer of Jaguar cars), and give them the ability to explore the car themselves.

We wanted people even to be able to ask questions and hear answers.

Stuart: Who did you select to see this experience?

Wheeler: We picked the usual and quite sceptical automotove journalists, along with some YouTube influencers, celebrities (we were in Los Angeles of course!) and, crucially, the tech media. We knew that the tech media were the people who were going to get this product in front of a whole wider audience than the usual automotive press – vital for launching something revolutionary like an electric car.

Stuart: What did the journalists see when they put on the headset?

Wheeler: The first thing they see is a Scalextric game, with E-Types and D-Types. This allowed people to become accustomed to the VR. You see, kids can throw on a headset and immediately 'get it' – they will start playing, exploring, interacting. Adults are very different – so we had to do something to warm them up. So they played Scalextric!

They could see each other's headsets and controllers, allowing people to wave at the people next to them in VR and see what each other was doing. Looking further away they could see the 30 people in London wave their controllers at them and they could wave back – with a tiny latency, around 1.1 second of latency.

Then you have a presenter appear, who is filmed live on a green screen. The presenter takes you away from where you are and into space, where double-decker buses fly past, along with flying pigs and then Ian Callum joins, talking about how the car was designed. He talks about how you have to throw everything away and start from a completely clean slate. He then draws out the car in front of the journalists. While he is doing this the journalists can individually control the model and move it and look around it.

Next the car is fully revealed, it is landed in the distance of the viewer's new perspective on the salt planes, before driving right up to you and nearly hitting you before going around you and driving off into the distance. Then you are back at the table, in the social environment, with the Head of Engineering, Ian Holburn, taking you through all the details of the car – exploding it, showing the batteries, the compartmentalization, wireless charging, etc. It is all breaking up, coming back together, driving along a map, driving into a garage.

We played a lot with scale, sometimes it was a tiny car coming down a mountain, demonstrating torque and acceleration. Another moment it's in a huge garage and you see the boot open and all the luggage piling in so you can visualize the space.

In virtual reality, you can do crazy and amazing stuff, but the job here was to tell a story. We had to give the journey key information, make the car look brilliant so we had to be sure to do this in a very linear way to make sure that the information was passed over.

Then there was the Q&A. You would have a question from London or Los Angeles or Germany – you could clearly hear Vinnie Jones or James Corden asking questions! Ian Callum would answer and you were like, WOW, there is a whole five-way conversation going on across two continents, with VIPs and a huge number of people listening. This really felt like the future. However, the problem at the moment is cost.

Luckily we managed to inspire Dell and HTC to work with us and Jaguar on it. They gave us all the kit. Otherwise this would never have been possible. This is a big problem with VR at the moment. Like so much new tech it is just too expensive at the beginning of its life cycle.

Stuart: Was the project considered a success?

Wheeler: One of the best car launches they have done.

Stuart: What was it about VR that made this project such a success?

Wheeler: An electric car is a very different proposition to a petrol car, without the engine, the drivetrain and the gearing, you've got none of the rules that have applied to the automotive industry for the last 100 years. You can move the cockpit forwards, you can put passengers in different positions, luggage can be in different places... The car does not even need to look like a car any more. Aerodynamically it has to work of course, but when you look at the car the bonnet is tiny compared to traditional cars.

Being able to break that down in a very visual way, without posters, projection or slides – VR really helped to facilitate that. Not to mention it was also cutting edge and so everyone was going to talk about it anyway.

Stuart: How much of this project was for PR and how much was for the practical benefits that VR brought?

Wheeler: There was only one car, so we could never have shown the car to as many journalists in as many different continents in such a detailed and engrossing way.

To illustrate this – my own personal point, something I noticed with some shock: this car had been launched for some time, it had been photographed, all the press work had been done, etc. One of the scenes that we did in VR – you actually got to sit in the interior of the car, Venice Beach appeared around you. You could move yourself around the interior of the car, even stand up and then look down on the car. You could see the texture of the dash, every single button etc.

The steering wheel appears in front of you and everyone, without fail, reaches out to hold it. I had this revelation about three months after the project ended – I never sat in the real car. I don't know why, I really should have. But I felt like I had, I just twigged, I've never sat in the real thing and I almost did not know!! I had convinced myself I had sat in the car because I had done it virtually. I knew every inch of that car from the inside, but all from VR.

So all these journalists would have had that same feeling, and that is so powerful. To feel that connected to a car that did not exist outside of one prototype.

Stuart: How did they measure the success of this?

Wheeler: JLR work with a company called Prime, a company that reports back on how many articles, words, film, TV coverage from any angle globally. I cannot give the exact data but this blew everything else out of the water in Los Angeles that year. The Germans were very f*cked off! If Mercedes, Audi and Porsche get annoyed then we're doing something right!

Stuart: What were the major challenges involved in making this project in VR terms?

Wheeler: Polygons. In order to get the quality into the renders, you want to put as many polygons as possible into the models. This gives you the detail, depth and reality to the models. The trouble is that if you overload it and you're trying to give so much information to people who are looking wherever they want, touching wherever they want, you get latency issues.

It was finding the fine balance of polygons – enough to make it look good and taking enough out to allow it to perform well.

Stuart: Is there a version that people can download and watch?

Wheeler: Yes, you can go to Vive Port and download the iPace Jaguar experience. It's nowhere near as sexy as what happened on the day, because you're not in a social environment with everything networked together.

Stuart: What about other platforms?

Wheeler: Not at this stage, 2017. I think it's on Oculus too but that's it – it was too cost prohibitive. We drew up something called the tunnel of immersion. If you've got Vive and Oculus at this end and Google Cardboard or 360 Video on a PC at the other end, there is a point where you are either making it for one end or the other and the two don't cross over. I know the VR industry promised that they would and that we wouldn't end up with a VHS and Betamax issue on our hands, but it does tend to exist.

We're making everything in real-time – Unity or Unreal. Trying to take that into Cardboard or even some of the Samsung headsets, it is not there yet. We have a massive project running at the moment though, called Quanta, which is going to allow us to broadcast into the metaverse. So we're going to have one virtual performance that can be pushed into every channel, whether that is on your phone or high-end VR headsets. This can be someone talking or singing, anything.

Right now, in 2017, it is very hard to justify marketing in VR if you are pushing to high-end headsets because the costs of content creation are just so high and the market size is so limited. Producing an experience for the 3 million or so people with these headsets, well you would be on a hiding to nowhere.

Until you get to the point where you have at least 50 million people using this stuff, it is pointless. This is where we are trying to push it into – you can have virtual content but you can consume that at different levels. From the creator's perspective they don't need to worry about creating it in multiple formats, which is where Quanta comes in – it can go out on phone, PC, 360 headsets, Google, full-on high end, etc. Sure you will get a different level but we only have to worry about broadcasting ones.

Stuart: Do you think VR is a valuable form of marketing?

Wheeler: I think right now, in 2017, no. There is no saturation level. Unless you quantify 360 as VR. I would be cautious to say don't do that, because you would be cheating people out of real VR experiences. People often think they have used VR when they have just seen 360 video. Well you really have not tried VR then, I think, and I'll try to get them into a proper VR experience, which then blows their minds!

I think we have to try to protect VR, in its purest form; it could easily be killed by saying it's 360 – it's not, it's so much more than that.

So the fair answer to the question is, right now, if I was a marketing director of a big brand, I would not go and spend huge amounts of money, unless I knew I was going to get a load of washed-up PR around the fact that it's super cool and the fact that I could break it down to 360 too, and get the view numbers. In the future it will be great marketing value.

Stuart: What will the future uses of VR be for marketing?

Wheeler: Everything. At Imagination we have always said that connecting someone to your product, whether that is a charity, a car, a phone, a coffee brand, whatever – getting people to feel that cup, pick up that phone, experience that drive is far more powerful in real life, one to one, than sticking up a billboard.

I think that the world has realized that – getting the people to experience the products directly is far more powerful. So where this will go is that everyone will realize that you can get your product instantly in front of someone, in the right setting. If you want me to appreciate where that coffee has come from then you can take me on a journey from the beans being harvested, to how they are roasted, into the machine as they are ground, maybe the smell is visualized around you, all the way to here is your hot coffee.

Here we see Wheeler clearly make the connection between experiential marketing and VR. In recent years, experiential has been seen as a huge growth area for marketing because, as Wheeler says, getting products in people's hands in the right setting generates tractions and ultimately sales. VR is the experiential of the future, it allows experiential to happen in the home.

INTERVIEW

Stuart: Is it the difference between seeing and feeling?

Wheeler: Yes, I think that's a really good way of putting it. There is something that happens to you in VR, where you feel it because your brain can be tricked and allow you to travel somewhere else virtually. I know that from playing some horrific horror game for the Vive. I was standing there at midnight, by myself, in the middle of my living room. My cat that was sitting on the sofa must have got freaked out, because he jumped on me.

My brain had totally transported me, I thought I was in that psychiatric ward until my cat, mercifully, broke the spell! That would never happen if I was watching TV or another format.

Stuart: What advice would you give to brands approaching VR for the first time?

Wheeler: Don't just use VR because it's cool, be cautious of people coming and selling you VR. I remember the same when social media took off, people saying they are social media experts after just one year. Everyone is suddenly a VR expert and you have all these film directors and everyone telling you they have done loads of stuff in VR – and you can find yourself in a pickle where you have just ended up making a very expensive film. You can easily spend too much money on the complications around the tech rather than focusing on the story.

Make sure you find people who really understand how to create things in Unreal or Unity, it's a very different approach.

You've got to also make sure that your content gets to the people you want it to. Original 360 content by Burberry on the catwalk was watched by about 30 people, which was fine for them at the time as the project was primarily for VR. We just did a project in China where 57 million people watched something live.

In summary, I would say, try starting with something small, don't spend a fortune. Make sure the story is there, don't just do it for the sake of doing something in VR.

Conclusions on the VR landscape

I think there are some fascinating perspectives and angles that the interviewees have revealed here. Below, I have highlighted some of the more salient points.

VR's reach has been extended by social 360 platforms

Corcoran highlighted the success of their South Africa Tourism VR project once it was posted as a 360 video on Facebook. At Visualise we have seen this time and time again, to the point that customers often come to us for social media-based 360 videos first and premium headset activations second/as a bonus.

User-generated and influencer-generated content is going to drive VR uptake

Corcoran has seen the explosion in influencer marketing and user-generated content (UGC) in other parts of advertising and thinks it is only a matter of time before the same thing happens to 360 video – driving VR uptake.

I also think this is a great opportunity for brands – to take an exciting emerging technology like 360/VR and combine it with creative and engaging influencers. There is huge potential there.

Virtual reality can be seen as a 'lean forward medium'

In the same way that trailers in cinemas have a customer's attention, VR is able to connect with people deeply, emotionally and in a memorable way.

Virtual reality lets you do anything you want

That is a pretty big statement, but really part of the magic. Imagine an experiential activation that lets you play football with your favourite Premiere League stars. Or one that lets you become an astronaut and do a space walk. These are amazing experiences that really wouldn't be possible in the real world. You can make your client's fantasies come true. What a powerful marketing tool that is.

So it is a medium, with great potential impact for brands.

VR allows for 'out of this world' experiences

Brands can use VR to give people VIP or out-of-this-world experiences that would be out of reach for most people in the real world. Whether that is being a character from the Marvel films, exploring underwater wrecks, going for a dinner date with your favourite band member or training with your favourite sports stars.

Rules for successful 360 content production

Nockles explains that there are a set of rules that have applied since the early days of the VR industry and these are still applicable today: close proximity, presenter led, engaging and intimate. Close proximity is often due to the lack of resolution in both cameras and headsets.

Presenter led just helps combat 'VR FOMO', basically aiding someone to follow a story through a scene and engaging them in the space.

Content in VR headsets is far more impactful than content outside headsets

You have a truly captive audience, their undivided attention. It is an incredibly natural, impactful medium. You can also show 360 content on mobile and desktop but the effect is not nearly as good.

VR needs to be social to flourish

Nockles believes that VR experiences need to allow communication and be social in order for the industry to truly take off. This is a vital point, right now – VR is perceived as isolating, it has the potential though to be one of the world's greatest social connectors.

VR's future is in real time

Nockles sees the natural evolution of 360 video being towards 'volumetric capture', allowing people to view content in a 'game engine' and walk around the film worlds, just like being an actual part of the film and on the set itself.

VR allows 'access'

Hood explains how VR gives people access to objects and places that they may not be able to physically get to (eg prototype cars, expensive, remote locations etc).

VR should be used when it solves a problem

It should not have a problem retrofitted to it in order to justify using VR. Something Hood highlights has happened too often in the industry so far. Wheeler also picks up on this point, saying you should do VR if there is a good story, not just for the sake of it.

VR still needs to hit a tipping point

Hood highlights that, for a lot of applications, clients still struggle to justify VR projects. The reason for this is simple – there are not enough headsets out there yet. The number of headsets needs to hit a tipping point to justify a lot of clients' spending. Wheeler also hits on this point, adding that we need to reach at least 50 million active users.

VR does not just let you see the product, it lets you feel it

It can really change opinions, make something stick in the mind and be memorable and even generate an emotional connection between a person and a brand. This fact mirrors the success in another part of marketing over the last decade, experiential. In experiential marketing, brands are trying to get their products into customers' hands; VR will let you do that but without even needing a physical product, or even location.

An important challenge to VR is shareability

People can have a great personal experience but then can find it hard to share. Experiences should be designed with sharing at their core in order to maximize ROI for brands/clients. Some of the most successful VR applications allow people to share personalized videos or photos of themselves in VR.

Headset cost is a limiting factor on VR

The cost of headsets is a perceived restriction on the growth/uptake of VR. From a campaign perspective it is a limiting factor on the number of 'eyeballs' that can see content. In the short/medium term, the workaround is 360 video with it being able to share online. Otherwise, the campaign has to have a targeted, physical activation with headsets supplied.

Types of virtual reality marketing and how to choose them

03

There are a number of different approaches you can take when using virtual reality (VR) for marketing. You will need to choose your delivery platform, headset, between interactive and passive and many more variants and iterations. We will look at the available and upcoming headsets, based on 2018, and bearing in mind that these will evolve very quickly. This chapter will give you a foundational understanding of the VR headsets available and coming soon, informing your choices of VR equipment and approach.

We will also revisit the choice of game engine-based versus 360 video-based content, also known as real-time engine versus VR film content.

Virtual reality headsets and platforms

There are hundreds of VR headsets in the market. The vast majority are based on the Google Cardboard system, ie they are simply holders for smartphones. The next most popular headsets are those that are also powered by smartphones but are integrated more deeply into the hardware – they have their own sensors and allow for a better VR experience than cardboard-based set-ups. Finally you have the high-end VR headsets that are tethered to a PC or console.

The sales figures, install base and much more, from all of these markets have been provided in Tables 3.1–3.4 by SuperData. This makes a fascinating insight into the health and growth of the market to date and into the future.

I think that the figures and predictions in Table 3.1 are fascinating. What you can see is a downward trend in overall VR headsets; however, don't be fooled. The number of headsets was bolstered early on by Google Cardboard, or 'light mobile' devices. These are often given out for free and rarely used more than once, so were in fact inflating early figures. The key thing is the massive growth in standalone headsets and consoles (predicted). SuperData actually predicts that sales will be going down in 2018 and beyond for PC headsets too, but I think the market will remain strong for people who want the kind of mindblowingly powerful VR experiences that only PCs can handle.

Table 3.2 looks in more detail at the specific brands of VR headsets and their sales in the last two years (2016–17). It is interesting to see the PC and console headsets growing their sales strongly but the premium mobile headsets in decline. This section of the industry is going to have a big boost soon though, from the launch of the Oculus Go and other standalone headsets.

Taking Google Cardboard out of the figures, in Table 3.3 we can see a clear predicted increase in VR – both shipments and, crucially, as an install base of users around the world. It is interesting to note how Asia has already overtaken Europe and America in both headset sales and install base.

Table 3.4 shows the revenue in sales of a number of really important items for the VR industry as a whole. Starting from the top, VR hardware will include all the headsets needed for VR, the software, all the games, films or professional VR applications bought and predicted to be bought from 2018 onwards. Interestingly you will notice that the software sales for mobile augmented reality are set to match the total sales of the VR industry. This is one of the ways we can visualize the meteoric rise of augmented reality that we are about to witness.

Also, it is interesting to see how strongly VR camera sales have increased, by 4.5 times from 2016 to 2017 as the medium is becoming

Table 3.1 Actual and predicted annual consumer shipments of the different classes of VR headsets

Annual consumer shipments	2016	2017	2018	2019	2020	2021
Light Mobile	84,398,503	59,313,844	38,847,040	21,911,663	15,498,275	9,209,110
Premium Mobile	5,064,463	4,063,069	2,704,765	1,870,568	1,553,462	1,179,192
Console	745,434	1,693,339	1,474,005	1,416,488	2,834,540	3,720,291
PC	828,316	1,391,826	516,949	345,734	234,360	219,412
Standalone	–	37,183	4,195,775	14,165,478	23,051,014	28,697,972
Total	**91,036,716**	**66,499,261**	**47,738,534**	**39,709,931**	**43,171,651**	**43,025,978**
Non-Cardboard Total	6,638,213	7,185,417	8,891,494	17,798,268	27,673,376	33,816,868

SOURCE SuperData Market Research, January 2018

Table 3.2 Actual headset shipments and industry research

Annual shipments	2016	2017
Oculus Rift	357,903	652,469
HTC Vive	420,108	531,412
Windows Mixed Reality	–	94,809
PlayStation VR	745,434	1,693,339
Samsung GearVR	4,512,732	2,006,150
Google Daydream	208,866	152,980
Google Cardboard	84,398,503	59,313,844

SOURCE Superdata Market Research, January 2018

more mainstream. More cameras mean more content, which in turn will drive more adoption.

SuperData classes Google Cardboard as a 'light mobile' VR headset, Samsung Gear VR and Google Daydream as a 'premium mobile' option. Oculus Rift, Windows MR and HTC Vive are 'PC' (ie they are tethered to a PC) and PlayStation VR as a 'console' option. Finally, as of 2018, there is a new class of 'Standalone' that includes the Oculus Go and the HTC Vive Focus. Let's look at each of these classes.

Light mobile VR headsets (Google Cardboard)

Google Cardboard-compatible headsets cost between $5 and $60, with basic, literally cardboard models at the cheaper end and headsets like the Zeiss VR One, which contain higher-quality lenses and construction, at the upper end. All of these headsets rely on the inbuilt sensors in the phones to positionalize your view and give the sense of immersion. Crucially Google Cardboard is the only VR platform that allows Apple iPhones. This is a huge benefit to the platform: Apple has not thrown their hat in the VR ring, so to reach those users, en masse, the only route is Google Cardboard.

Due to the nature and price of Google Cardboard materials they can be custom printed/branded. This has led to a huge number of

Table 3.3 Region-level (without Google Cardboard)

Regional consumer shipments	2016	2017	2018	2019	2020	2021
North America	2,274,232	2,182,738	2,705,871	5,453,367	8,226,454	10,105,842
Europe	1,918,520	1,702,598	2,110,421	4,121,105	6,231,726	7,624,082
Asia	1,592,111	2,692,990	3,271,559	6,731,189	10,859,524	13,206,176
Latin America	468,517	357,288	502,050	957,617	1,570,385	1,922,937
Rest of World	384,834	249,803	301,593	534,989	785,287	957,830
Total	**6,638,213**	**7,185,417**	**8,891,494**	**17,798,268**	**27,673,376**	**33,816,868**

Regional install base	2016	2017	2018	2019	2020	2021
North America	2,239,530	3,885,918	4,766,365	8,069,209	12,900,922	19,510,777
Europe	1,889,246	3,031,126	3,717,484	6,097,895	9,772,741	14,719,384
Asia	1,567,817	4,794,317	5,762,818	9,959,970	17,030,165	25,496,418
Latin America	461,368	636,077	884,356	1,416,962	2,462,716	3,712,506
Rest of World	378,962	444,722	531,253	791,610	1,231,506	1,849,229
Total	**6,536,924**	**12,792,160**	**15,662,276**	**26,335,646**	**43,398,050**	**65,288,314**

SOURCE SuperData Market Research, 2018

Table 3.4 XR revenue and forecasts

Virtual reality revenue ($)

	2016	2017	2018	2019	2020	2021
Hardware	1,613,728,922	1,965,397,068	2,862,148,304	6,577,997,711	9,791,749,568	12,160,135,683
Software	227,717,952	554,316,868	1,017,109,514	2,079,269,450	3,650,181,200	5,567,100,428
Total	**1,841,446,874**	**2,519,713,935**	**3,879,257,819**	**8,657,267,162**	**13,441,930,768**	**17,727,236,111**

Mobile augmented reality revenue ($)

	2016	2017	2018	2019	2020	2021
Hardware	–	–	–	–	–	–
Software	925,594,332	1,066,345,769	2,173,887,204	6,492,787,651	10,607,218,267	17,401,888,481
Total	**925,594,332**	**1,066,345,769**	**2,173,887,204**	**6,492,787,651**	**10,607,218,267**	**17,401,888,481**

Mixed and augmented reality headset revenue ($)

	2016	2017	2018	2019	2020	2021
Hardware	91,078,000	96,493,280	382,020,588	2,666,720,879	6,597,491,292	12,025,432,544
Software	9,864,340	53,403,409	65,088,086	297,922,240	1,037,087,899	2,920,363,896
Total	**100,942,340**	**149,896,689**	**447,108,674**	**2,964,643,120**	**7,634,579,191**	**14,945,796,440**

360 camera revenue ($)

	2016	2017	2018	2019	2020	2021
Totals	112,411,080	529,164,053	1,689,635,208	1,758,321,648	2,265,554,282	2,795,535,395

Total revenue ($)

	2016	2017	2018	2019	2020	2021
Hardware	1,817,218,002	2,591,054,400	4,933,804,100	11,003,040,239	18,654,795,143	26,981,103,623
Software	1,163,176,623	1,674,066,046	3,256,084,805	8,869,979,341	15,294,487,365	25,889,352,805
Total	**2,980,394,626**	**4,265,120,446**	**8,189,888,905**	**19,873,019,580**	**33,949,282,508**	**52,870,456,428**

SOURCE SuperData Market Research, 2018

marketing activations where VR headsets can be mailshot to the target market or handed out at trade fairs or points of sale. The headsets often come flat packed, allowing for postage. One of our projects at Visualise, with the *Financial Times*, called Hidden Cities, saw them posting headsets to thousands of their subscribers to accompany a piece that was being launched in their weekend magazine (Figure 3.1).

The main drawback with Google Cardboard is performance. You are relying on inbuilt sensors in the phones, you have to allow for backwards compatibility of older phones and people's phones often have other, memory-hogging apps open. All of this adds up to more lag in the experiences and therefore more likelihood of motion sickness. Another drawback is the comfort and build quality of the headsets and lenses. Particularly at the cheaper end, most of the headsets don't even have straps, meaning they have to be constantly held up like a pair of binoculars, which is not indusive to longer experiences.

Related again to performance, as you typically build Google Cardboard apps to work on the maximum number of different type

Figure 3.1 Google Cardboard headsets from Visualise's campaign with Adam&EveDDB and the FT

SOURCE photo reproduced courtesy of FT (June 2016)

and age of phones, you often are restricted to the performance of the lower common denominator. What this means practically is that there is very limited processor or graphics power for interactive VR experiences. So if you are running something that requires a game engine, the graphics need to be incredibly simple to allow for the phone to run the content smoothly. This often means that interactive VR is overlooked, in favour of 360 video-based experiences, which can run at a relatively high quality. This then opens up another bonus feature, unique to 360 video, if the user does not have a VR headset, they can just view the content full screen on their phone and still use the inbuilt gyroscope to allow them to move the phone around themselves to explore the footage. This feature is quite brilliantly called 'magic window'.

There are a number of ways to view content on Google Cardboard headsets. The simplest, and cheapest, way is to simply upload a 360 video to YouTube and then view it using the YouTube app on iPhone or Android. Next is to make a web page with either WebVR or a 360 video player. Finally, the premium option, dedicated apps.

YouTube

A 360 video, shot/produced for a brand or company can be uploaded to YouTube; this means that, if viewing on the YouTube app, people can watch the content in VR, through Google Cardboard. This has a number of benefits: 1) the content is also available for people without Google Cardboard headsets on any platform, including desktop and mobile; 2) there is no charge from YouTube, so it is essentially a free way of reaching an audience; 3) YouTube is 3D and ambisonic audio enabled – meaning a higher-quality content can be viewed in its near-best form.

The real problem comes from how people access this footage – the YouTube app is not installed as standard on iPhones. So people would have to download the app first, and then follow a link to the content or search for the content in YouTube. On Android devices it is a little bit more straightforward – the app is pre-installed, allowing less friction in accessing the content. So if people receive a headset with a link on it that is either QR code or plain text, they will

Figure 3.2   YouTube screengrab from *Dublin in the Dark*, a film by Visualise and Adam&EveDDB for the FT (Nov 2016) (Google Cardboard icon can be seen in the bottom right-hand corner)

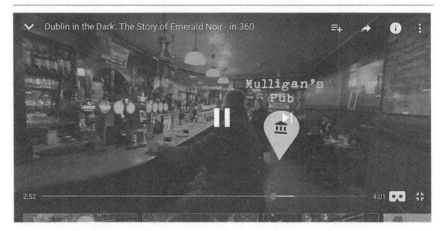

instantly reach the content on Android but not on iOS. There is also one more barrier – users need to click a little icon in the bottom-right corner of the view in order to launch the split-window version of the content (Figure 3.2).

WebVR and Web 360

WebVR describes the new online platform, based on JavaScript, that allows you to use VR headsets, including Oculus Rift, HTC Vive and Google Cardboard, through a web browser. For interactive pieces, even high-end smartphones have a laggy experience, in my opinion, so I prefer to use web-based VR for 360 video application.

The attraction to Web 360 is that users just need to have a single link and then they can access and view content on Cardboard without having to install an app. You could even default the viewer to a Cardboard split-screen view. The player itself can also be customized however you or the brand/client would like, not just in how it looks, but even in the quality of the content that is streamed.

A drawback with Web 360 is that the content has to be hosted somewhere and that carries a cost – especially if your content goes viral, you can find yourself or the client faced with a large bill for their success! So be sure to understand the full cost implications of your content before pushing it live. Another issue of course is that, unlike YouTube, the webpage/web app will need to be built, which will of course carry a cost.

Google Cardboard apps

The best way to view content on Google Cardboard headsets is with a dedicated app. An app allows for the branding and message surrounding the content to be controlled and also allows for greater control of the quality of the content than you would have in WebVR or YouTube. In the apps we make at Visualise we often give two options for viewing content – download or stream, with download being the optimal quality. As you are not running the content in a browser you don't have the other 'overhead' running in the background that WebVR does; it is also custom branded, unlike YouTube. As with Web 360 though, the content has to be hosted somewhere, which is a cost to consider. If you are building an interactive VR app for Cardboard, then you will have more control and optimization over performance than you would with WebVR. There will also be a cost associated with designing, building and updating any app.

Google Cardboard summary

Overall, the fact that Google Cardboard is cheap and allows cross-platform compatibility (Apple phones included) means that this is often the most common choice for VR experiences for brands. They can produce a piece of 360 video content that goes online, reaching millions of people, and is also viewed on VR headsets through the Google Cardboard platform. If you are looking to use influencers and leverage the reach they create, then the Google Cardboard VR platform is a top choice (alongside Facebook 360 – more on that later).

Premium mobile VR headsets

In this category we have the Samsung GearVR and Google Daydream headsets. Both of these are powered by a user's smartphone. This is placed in the front of the headset, becoming the screen and the power behind the experience. The benefit to this approach is primarily in cost – if the user already has a high-end smartphone such as the Samsung Galaxy S7 or S8, or the Google Pixel 1 or 2, then they can buy a headset for around $60–$100 and have a brilliant VR experience.

Built in to the phone-powered, premium-mobile headsets are gyroscopes and accelerometers that greatly advance the phone's ability to positionalize the headset and provide smooth, comfortable motion. They are also built for exact phones, rather than allowing backwards compatibility to all phones – this means the experiences can run at higher speeds, hence a better quality of footage and comfort. The headsets also come with a controller, allowing footage to be easily navigated and interactive games to be more easily controlled.

This level of phone is most commonly used in brand activations based on 360 video, in particular the Samsung GearVR. The first main advantage to using this system is its balance between cost and quality – for a total of around $700 you can have the phone, headset and a pair of headphones. Compare that to the $1,500 to $2,000 you need for the top-level headsets and their accompanying computer. The difference in quality for 360 video content between the premium mobile and PC headsets is relatively small.

The premium mobile, phone-based VR headsets have a number of other attractions when it comes to VR activations for brands. They are able to be packed down into small cases and easily transported, and they are simple to operate – launch the app and place the phone in the headset. They also do not require a separate computer with a cable tethering the two together.

Where the premium mobile headsets really struggle though is in the interactive content, based on game engines. The content is incredibly processor intensive and also really suits full motion-tracked controllers and head tracking. Mobile phone processors simply do not have the power to give justice to these kinds of experiences. Hence, if you are doing any marketing activity and want it to be interactive (such as the growing trend in industrial machine walkarounds at trade shows) then your product is going to look far better in a PC-powered premium headset.

Samsung GearVR

The Samsung GearVR is the result of a partnership between Samsung and Oculus, it is also sometimes called the Oculus Mobile. The GearVR can run from an S7, S8 or S9 Galaxy phone and is now in it's third generation. Marketing content made for this platform is difficult to get in the main, Oculus, ecosystem. The reason for this is that Oculus does not want overt advertising to flood the platform. So unless it is subtle sponsorship of an experience the content needs to be private – ie just downloaded on phones that have a particular Oculus member login associated with the app. Another way of getting content on to the phone is simply to upload an 'APK' (Android Package Kit).

The APKs just need to be 'signed' for each phone they are going to be on – this means finding a unique code to the phone and then ensuring this is logged in the code of the app itself, therefore allowing the app to launch on that phone. As you can see, this is quite a painful process, so thankfully Oculus allowed for private apps to be uploaded and shared to specific Oculus usernames through the Oculus store, rather than directly.

When using the GearVR in events, typically a spare phone is charged while one is in use, meaning constant use can be maintained during busy periods in activations. For some VR applications you need to be careful of headsets overheating, less of a problem on the newer Galaxy phones but certainly an issue on the S6s. Some producers used to custom-mount fans on to the headsets to keep them cool. We once added customer-branded logos to the back of all our phones during one activation and found this had the unfortunate effect of making them overheat fairly quickly!

GearVR headsets are used more than any other VR headset for activations – this is due to their balance in cost and the performance they deliver. Particularly when it comes to 360 video. They can play the video at a high resolution and on a screen that is the same resolution as the premium headsets. This means that for a third of the price of a premium set-up (eg Oculus Rift, plus gaming PC) you can give the same experience. Plus, you are not tethered to a computer and it is a lot easier to set up, post to another activation and run.

I would not advise using the GearVR for game-engine or interactive-based activations though. As it is only running from a mobile phone, it does not have the horsepower to display high-quality, interactive graphics and gameplay – that is unless the program is really well optimized and relatively simple.

Google Daydream View

A similar platform to Oculus Mobile, Daydream is Google's premium space for VR content, accessed through their brilliant Daydream View headsets (Figure 3.3). It is designed to be device agnostic, accepting Google's Pixel 1 and 2 and other high-end Android smartphones, including the Samsung Galaxy S8, S8+, Samsung Galaxy Note8, Samsung Galaxy S9, S9+ and LG V30. One of the key features of the Google Daydream View is its fabric-covered construction and lightweight build. It is incredibly comfortable, and in its second iteration has improved heat dissipation, lenses and ergonomics.

Standalone headsets

The Oculus Go was released in May 2018 and is the first in the next generation of totally dedicated VR kits that are independent of

Figure 3.3   Google Daydream View headset (2017)

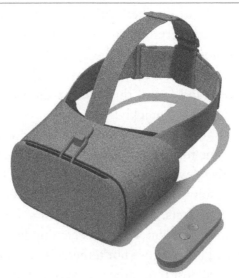

SOURCE Image courtesy of Google

Figure 3.4   The Oculus Go, standalone VR headset

SOURCE   Image courtesy of Oculus (2018)

computers or phones. The Vive Focus, from HTC, was not released at the time of writing, but also looks to be a very compelling option. Crucially, the Vive Focus will also allow for six degrees of freedom, ie you will be able to walk around the content!

Oculus Go

The Oculus Go (Figure 3.4) is probably going to have the biggest impact on the VR market since the original Oculus was announced on Kickstarter in 2011. The Go will retail at around $200, and requires no other peripherals, mobile phones, computers or even headphones. I expect it to be hugely popular and to pave the way for a viable consumer market to be targeted, in VR, in the home. From a software perspective, it runs from the same system as the GearVR, so it has launched with the same apps and programs from the off, and this should help it get a running start.

PC VR headsets

It is with the PC VR headsets (aka premium VR headsets) that the ultimate quality in VR is reached. Full, interactive VR, with high-resolution graphics and low latency, and positional tracking, allowing people to move through content with six degrees of freedom. You have to experience VR at some point on a top-level headset – it is really incomparable to all other levels. For 360 video too, PC headsets allow a higher resolution of content to be played in 3D, allowing for the best quality.

I will introduce the current crop of top-level headsets, as at the start of 2018. There are a huge number of headsets available, so this is not an exhaustive list, but more highlights, starting from the lower-level price points and moving up.

Windows 'mixed reality' headsets

At the lower price point we have the Windows 'mixed reality' headsets (Figure 3.5). These headsets are all manufactured to the Microsoft specification for their new VR platform. They are called 'mixed reality' but they are not, they are simply virtual reality. Each headset has a pair of sensors on the front that allow it to detect its position in 3D space.

Prices of these headsets vary from $350 to $500, and they also require, as with all other premium headsets, a PC to be plugged into. This PC has to be a high-spec gaming machine, with a processor and GPU that will be able to cope with the performance requirements of the medium.

At Visualise, we have always used Oculus Rift, Samsung GearVR and HTC Vive for our physical activations, originally because these were the only headsets available, so I have not personally road tested these headsets. However, the fact that they have 'inside out' tracking

Figure 3.5   Asus Windows 'mixed reality' headset and controllers

SOURCE Image courtesy of Asus (2018)

is a big advantage from the ease of set-up point of view. Anecdotally, they are very easy to work with, fast to set up and robust.

The Windows mixed reality headsets have 'inside out tracking'. This is the ability for a headset to detect its position in a room, without the need for external tracking sensors. With both the Oculus Rift and the HTC Vive, you need to set up sensors in the room and calibrate them, which is tricky sometimes and an added pressure if time is of the essence! The fact that the Microsoft headsets don't need to do this is a big advantage and is the way that all headsets will be moving in the future.

The Oculus Rift

The originator of this entire wave of VR, the industry has a lot to thank Oculus for. Its visionary, and controversial, founder, Palmer Luckey launched a Kickstarter project that famously reached over 1,000 per cent of its funding in 2012. Oculus went through a series of developer kits, learning over five years how to make excellent VR headsets. Their first kit was called the DK1 (Development Kit 1), followed by the DK2, and then the long-awaited consumer version, the CV1. The CV1 is now available with Oculus's 'touch' controllers, allowing you to interact naturally and intuitively with the world around you (see Figures 3.6 and 3.7).

Figure 3.6   Oculus Rift Headset, top ¾ view

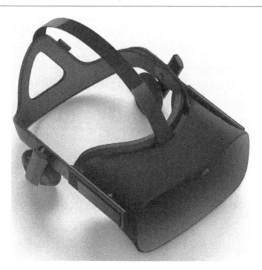

SOURCE Image courtesy of Oculus (2018)

Figure 3.7   Oculus Rift 'touch' controllers

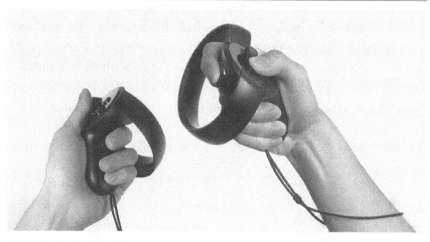

SOURCE Image courtesy of Oculus (2018)

Retailing at $399, the Oculus Rift is a very well-priced headset for what you get. It is very comfortable, with a good resolution and high-quality build. We use them day in day out at Visualise and have been highly impressed in their robustness over time and constant use. From the perspective of activations, they have built in headphones, which means less tangling of wires and much better ease of use. They require sensors to be set up to allow for room-scale tracking, which can be a little finickity to get right and can be a small frustration.

HTC Vive

The Vive is a hugely impressive headset. The most premium of the PC headsets, retailing at $599, it was the first of the headsets to allow for six degrees of freedom (full room-scale VR). The screen, the lenses and the build quality are excellent. It ships with two hand controllers, which, whilst large are very intuitive and soon disappear as you become immersed in the content.

HTC partnered with Steam early on and quickly built a market off the back of this prolific gaming platform. Despite being more expensive than the Oculus Rift, the Vive has led the race for sales (see Table 3.2). This is in equal parts due to its partnership with Steam, its first mover advantage in room-scale VR and its excellent build quality and general use experience.

HTC has recently announced the Vive Pro; this incredible headset has built-in headphones, the option for a wireless adapter (allowing you to be free of the tether to your computer) and a higher-resolution display. The cameras on the front of the headset (Figure 3.8) allow you to see through the headset into the room, through the 'Chaperone' system (Figure 3.9).

Figure 3.8   The HTC Vive Pro

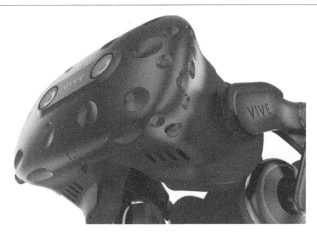

SOURCE Image courtesy of HTC Vive (2018)

Figure 3.9   The HTC Vive Pro, side view

SOURCE Image courtesy of HTC Vive (2018)

Figure 3.10   An HTC Vive Tracker

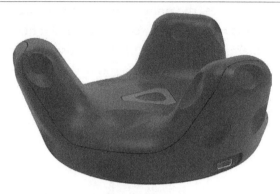

SOURCE Image courtesy of HTC Vive (2018)

The retail cost for the Pro will, no doubt, be higher, but the price point has not been announced yet. No doubt the Pro will be coveted for VR activations and private use alike. It will certainly allow HTC to maintain its reputation as the best headset for professional use, if money is no object!

One of the other unique and brilliant features of the Vive is the production of 'trackers' (Figure 3.10). You add these to items/body parts that you want to be tracked in the interactive world, for example on to a piece of sports equipment such as a baseball bat or cricket bat. Having the tracker on the item means it can appear in the interactive world.

Pimax 8K

Yes, 8K, you read it right! One of the big objections that first-time users have with VR is the fact that you can still clearly see pixels. The Pimax is a big step away from that with its 8K headset (Figure 3.11). Well, when you dig a little deeper it is actually 4k per eye... And then dig deeper, it is 3,840 pixels per eye... That is still fairly impressive – compare that to the current Oculus Rift, which is 2,160 pixels per eye, and you can see it is a huge jump up.

The Pimax also has a very wide field of view, ie you don't see the black border to the content so easily to the left and right of the view. This 200-degree field of view, though, means the pixels are spread over a futher space, reducing the effect of higher resolution. It is still

Figure 3.11   Pimax 8K Headset

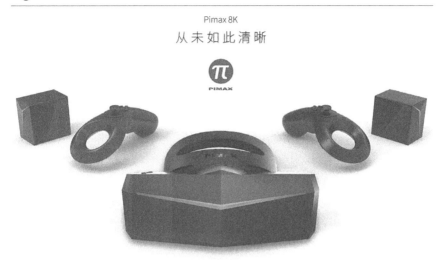

Pimax 8K

从 未 如 此 清 晰

SOURCE   Image courtesy of Pimax VR (2018)

going to be better, however, just not as much of an improvement, as they are also pushing the field of view.

More pixels of course need more power so you will need a very powerful workstation PC to have it working at its best. The Pimax 8K started as a Kickstarter project and, as often happens with Kickstarter projects, there have been significant delays in manufacturing: we hope to see this in the hands of consumers and marketers in the second half of 2018.

Types of virtual reality

Now that we have established the different types of VR headsets, we can be more informed on the types of VR and how to choose them. As mentioned in earlier stages of this book, VR is broadly broken into two sections – interactive and non-interactive. These are in their own right very broad terms. Let's look at each of them and drill down.

Interactive VR

Interactive VR are experiences that let you do more than just look around them; you can interact with the experience to varying degrees.

At one end of the scale could be a 'room scale' experience on the HTC Vive, where the user can walk around a product, interacting with it. Imagine a jet engine hovering in front of you: you can walk around it and grab different parts (where indicated) and pull these off or out of the way, revealing the workings within. Perhaps there is a button you can press and the whole engine explodes outwards showing all of its component parts floating around you, or you could pull a throttle lever and see it roar to life in front of you, spitting flames! On the other hand, interactivity could be very simple: imagine a 360 video that follows a band to the stage of a gig; just before you go on stage it asks you – do you want to be the singer, drummer or guitarist – and the video plays on after your choice from that perspective.

So both of the above examples are interactive, but to vastly varying degrees. The level of interactivity required will be determined by the product or service you are selling, your required reach and your budget. For the majority of interactive pieces though, you are essentially making a computer game – you are building the experience in a game engine or a 'real-time' engine. Typical real-time engines for VR are Unity and Unreal. These powerful systems allow you to create virtual environments of anything you could imagine.

If you are going down the interactive route it is worth bearing in mind that the best graphics and visual fidelity require a lot of processor power – so if you have a product like the engine mentioned above, that needs to look visually stunning, then you will need to choose your system wisely. This usually means opting for Oculus Rift or HTC Vive. What you will have is incredibly impressive and will blow people away at trade shows or activations. It is important though that you think about reach. How are you going to reach people beyond the premium headsets?

There are usually a couple of ways of tackling reach with interactive VR. You can produce a simplified version of the experience for Google Cardboard headsets, lower poly, no six degrees of freedom, less interactivity, etc. This way, you can order hundreds or thousands of custom-branded Google Cardboard headsets and send them or give them away to potential customers. You will still have your premium activation, just another, secondary way of getting the content in the hands of more people.

Another way to reach more people with the content is to produce an 'on rails' version of the experience that is 360 video – allowing people to see the content, look around themselves, but not actually click on things or interact with them. Whilst a long second best from the fully interactive version, this could act as a taster, encouraging people to come to the activation or just allowing that many more people to see your innovative project even if they don't have a headset (360 video can be viewed online and on Facebook and YouTube without a headset).

At the highest end of the interactive VR product line are experiences like 'The Void', their recent collaboration with *Star Wars*, through Industrial Light and Magic's 'X Lab'. This truly remarkable experience is, technically, marketing for the *Star Wars* mega brand, but through the eyes of any of the legion of fans who have tried it... it is living their fantasies. When you start the experience you are fitted with an interactive vest, a custom headset, with built-in headphones and a flip visor. You meet your real-life teammates before flipping down the visor and being introduced into the magical world of the *Star Wars* universe.

In VR, the other players are storm troopers, they look real, you can see where they are looking, what they are doing, you can talk to them! With your team you have to take on the rescue of a secret artefact from the Empire. You are walking through spaceships, over lava flows on moving platforms, pressing real buttons to open doors or to solve problems. You pick up some guns and start being involved in the most almighty shootout imaginable. It is incredible fun. I happily walked away lighter by £30 from Westfield in London – and by the looks of the queues, a lot of other people were equally happy.

Surely this is the dream for any marketing project, to also make money from the activity itself, but this is very rarely possible. The cost of building an experience like 'The Void' must have been huge, from a physical build and location-rental perspective but also from a game development and R&D perspective. What you have though is an experience that shows the future potential for VR – where you collaborate/play in incredible other worlds, with friends anywhere in the world, and are part of the film, rather than a passive observer.

Interactive is going to be huge, it is going to be escapism on another level far beyond anything other than The Void allows today. On a global reach scale though, it is going to need a high-end headset, computer and haptic suit in as many houses in the world as possible. We've got a way to go for that! In the meantime, bring the technology to the people, set up in malls, stations, high footfall areas, or create events around the content, inviting press, your industry and influencers.

360 Video

360 video, also known as VR film, is a very versatile medium, and very different to interactive VR. Like traditional videos or films you are watching – it is more 'passive' than interactive VR. 360 video has been incredibly popular for marketing, for the following reasons: 1) it is relatively cost effective to produce; 2) it can reach people outside of those with headsets (ie you can view it on your desktop or phone too); 3) it is platform agnostic (interactive VR often has to be produced as a specific app for a specific platform).

Although passive, when viewed in a headset, there are a number of features of 360 video that greatly differentiate it from traditional 16×9 format film. One of the key differences is the physicality of the experience. By this I mean the fact that your body/mind is partly tricked by what you are seeing and so there is a different relationship to the content. For example, a shot hanging from a drone over a city could give you vertigo, or people moving too close to the camera could make you want to take a step back. It is the fact that people have a one-to-one relationship with the content – ie the camera is the viewer – that makes this medium so powerful (and so tricky to execute well!).

Another interesting feature is breaking the fourth wall – ie the actors talking to you – which raises the question, who are you? Can you be a part of the scene that is integral to the story or are you just a fly on the wall? As mentioned earlier in the book, Oculus Story Studio called the conundrum of not being able to influence the environment and yet being part of it the 'Swayze effect'. This ability to play with users' sense of self is a powerful tool in the armoury of VR marketers. It leads to a huge array of possible unique experiences and something that all clients love – world's firsts.

Of course, 360 video will look best on higher-resolution headsets. Right now, we can shoot the content at a higher resolution than it can be played back, so to show it at its best, go for an Oculus Rift, HTC Vive or, if you can get hold of them, a Pimax 8K! Next best option is the Samsung GearVR or the Google Daydream View. All of these will work brilliantly at experiential set ups, trade shows, etc. You can add in extra physical stimulations too, as with a piece of footage that Visualise shot for Unit 9 and Wimbledon, which allowed you to fly, lying face down on a platform, looking down over Wimbledon below. While you were doing this, a series of fans were blowing air at you, hugely adding to the feeling of flight.

Outside of experiential, we have done some pieces that are just launched to the public VR platforms, such as *The Economist* VR (Google Cardboard, Dayream and Oculus) and our piece for Facebook and the Van Gogh Museum, which went on Oculus Mobile. Often, until premium headset numbers pick up, this stage is skipped, in favour of a secondary launch of the video on Google Cardboard, which can mean a dedicated app for iOS and Android or a simple upload to YouTube.

Implementing social virtual reality marketing

One of the biggest barriers to using VR in marketing is its perceived inability to being social. Customers are in solo experiences, in head-sets; they apparently cannot easily share that experience. Well, you will be pleased to hear that there are a number of ways of making VR social and shareable – well, didn't Facebook buy Oculus for $2 billion?! In this section, we are going to look at making VR social in physical activations, in consumer downloaded VR apps and in 360 videos.

Physical activations

If you are aiming to reach customers with physical activations in store or in public areas, then you need to build a system that both enables and encourages sharing. In an activation's simplest form it is a headset that someone puts on, they have an experience and then leave the experience. That individual may have a great time, but the only way they are sharing it is by talking about it on social platforms or directly to their contacts. There needs to be a mechanic that allows people to easily share their experience.

Funnily enough, one of the best ways I saw this done was one of the first public VR experiences I ever tried – Marriott Hotels in New York.[1] This was a hugely ambitious experience, by Framestore, that combined 3D 360 video with CG, had customers in specially made experience booths and rumbled the floor, blew sea mist at them and more. While people were queuing for their turn, they filled out their details in an iPad – name, e-mail address, etc. This was a stipulation of using the experience. The brand ambassador would then help the customer into the booth, get them suited up and let them at it!

While in the experience, the computer running it would log where the user was looking and actually save a video view of their experience – where they were looking, in 16×9 format. This video, with a pre-filled out e-mail, was then sent to the customer, thereby giving them an easily shared asset. It is not just your view that can be shared though, a link to the whole experience as a 360 video could also be shared. The beauty of sharing this 360 asset is that it is already on a social platform, eg Facebook or YouTube.

This idea can be taken to a brilliant extreme – using green screens, you can give people a video of themselves immersed in the virtual environment! Watch the video of Mat Smith from Engaget, surrounded by a green screen and then by the world he is seeing, immersed in the headset.[2] Particularly for the more interactive games and stunts in VR, such as walking the plank between two tall towers for example, you are going to get some very entertaining and shareable footage!

Arguably not a marketing experience but a piece of entertainment that makes its own revenue, The Void (*Star Wars* experience) shows you how social VR can be. You play in the *Star Wars* universe with other people, live, there with you. You all look like storm troopers but can speak to one another, shoot one another and help one another, whatever you prefer! It is amazing how quickly you forget that you are in a game, and just act and react and interact like the real world.[3]

One of the more recent, and successful, social VR marketing applications was the Jaguar launch of the I-Pace (see Chapter 2 and the interview with Ross Wheeler for a deeper dive). In this experience, presenters from Jaguar were live streamed into the VR environment, to present the car, live, to journalists all over the world. This hugely ambitious project allowed everyone to speak to each other, hear each other's questions and interact with the environment.

Social VR experiences

Above and beyond the physical activations, what about if you are a brand that releases an app on to some of the available VR platforms such as Steam VR or Oculus? Well, there are options for these to be social – I don't just mean shareable but actually social. There are a number of social platforms out there, including vTime, Viso Places and Facebook's own spaces. Where all of these struggle at present though is in the number of users – ie the community being big enough to justify these experiences.

This issue of the number of users holding back the more social experiences is only temporary, as the number of people with VR headsets grows so will the application for social VR marketing experiences. There is of course, in the meantime, opportunities for brands to associate themselves with social experiences in VR, such as shared music concerts or live sporting events.

The simplest social VR experiences on mobile allow users to teleport around chat rooms or spaces by using their headset's 'gaze' mechanic (aka 'look to select'), they will see other users as avatars and can approach them and start chatting. The simplest brand involvement would be branding the 360 areas people are chatting in, for a start, but then moving on to putting on live events in the virtual world that people can interact with and participate in. These events could be a conversation or interview with someone famous, eg Stephen Spielberg in conversation with Ernest Cline in a 3D model of the caravan from the film *Ready Player One* (hint – it is all about VR – I mention this book, and now film, a lot and strongly recommend you read/watch it[4]).

All VR headsets have the ability to be social, they all have microphones and speakers, the minimum you need. In mobile-based headsets like Google Cardboard and Samsung GearVR, the device is actually powered by a phone, the most social of all our technologies! So it is just a case of having the right idea and critical mass to have a social marketing success in VR.

VR on social platforms

So how can VR be used on existing social platforms? Well, there is one very straightforward way – 360 video. YouTube and Facebook have been supporting 360 video for a while now, allowing professionals and the public alike to upload immersive content to the platform. More recently still, they have allowed live streaming of 360 content (more on that later in the book). Allowing 360 videos on social platforms all of a sudden opened up the world of VR to everyone else, without a headset. It was one of the most important moments in the evolution and uptake of VR content worldwide. Crucially, brands could spend on marketing material in VR (360 video) and have it reach millions of people above and beyond those with headsets.

How to choose your approach

The kind of VR you need to choose will depend on the product you are selling, where the promotion is going to be used, the kind of impact you need to make and the budget you have to play with. Looking back to Chapter 2 and the interview with Ross Wheeler, we saw how a large, premium car brand used VR to solve a number of problems: 1) they only had one physical prototype; 2) they wanted to steal the show from other competitors and get journalists talking; 3) they wanted to show the car in a way that suited its next-generation technology.

The above is a far cry from when Audi asked us to film their new TTRS in Germany at their test track, there was also just one (right-hand drive) prototype there. Audi's particular need was to practically show people the new car and let them experience its speed, whilst understanding the principles of its design. You could have done this with interactive, but it would have been a significant amount more expensive and you wouldn't have the charming Jürgen Löffler sitting next to you!

The longer tail of the experience is important too – can the resulting VR be reused, how much will it cost to set up again in a showroom and what kind of service contract will be needed to train staff? Audi's content was part of a series of 360 videos made about a number of their cars. They had racing seats set up at dealerships and a dedicated app where people could choose their experience. Setting up a fully tracked and interactive experience like that of the Jaguar one would be a far harder task.

Notes

1 Framestore (2014) [accessed 8 April 2018] Marriott Hotels VR experience [Online] http://framestorevr.com/marriott/

2 Smith, M (31 May 2016) [accessed 8 April 2018] Looking inside an HTC Vive game using a green screen, Engadget [Online] https://www.youtube.com/watch?v=BjdzsVFs2C0

3 The Void and Industrial Light and Magic (11 October 2017) [accessed 8 April 2018] Star Wars: Secrets of the Empire – The Void and ILMxLAB – Hyper-Reality Experience [Online] https://www.youtube.com/watch?v=Oad_t6k3w5c

4 Wikipedia [accessed 8 April 2018] Ernest Clien, Ready Player One (2011) [Online] https://en.wikipedia.org/wiki/Ready_Player_One

Virtual reality production   04

How to make VR

Virtual reality (VR) production spans both 360 video (VR films) and interactive VR. For both forms of VR you need to go through stages of pre-production and planning before you can begin production.

In 360 video, production means the actual capture of the content. Post-production means the crafting, editing and creation of the story after the capture. In interactive VR, production means the building of the interactive piece in its entirety.

Pre-production

Before diving into a VR project or production, you need to deeply understand the reasoning behind making the project and the necessary outcomes. It is vital that the project has a vision that is understood by both the content creator (the agency) and the client.

Before we come to a vision, there are a few things you have to establish when planning a VR production:

- What problem is this solving (**Why**)?
- **Who** do you want to see this?
- **What** do you want people to see, feel and do?
- **How** do you want them to see this? ('How' being a particular constraint of VR now.)

After these foundations are set it is good to establish some key performance indicators (KPIs) that the project can be benchmarked against.

The next step is developing the **creative, storyboarding** and **scripting**. This is followed by the practical steps of **planning and logistics** (360 video) or setting up of product backlog and **sprints** (interactive VR).

Why: *what problem are we solving?*

First, let's establish why we are doing a VR project at all!

Take a look at this with an example, Audi, and a project we completed for them in 2015. The first thing we want to ask or understand is 'what is the business problem' or opportunity that the client wants to solve? Audi came to us on the launch of the TTRS, the sporty end of their TT range. The car was soon to be launched in the UK but they did not have a production version of the car available for showrooms. So they wanted to find a way to stimulate pre-sales before the car had rolled off the ferry.

In this case, there was a clear problem and the client had already identified that VR could be the solution. By producing a virtual version of the car we would be able to bring it to customers before they could actually touch the real thing.

This is a very obvious one, but establishing which problem it is that you are solving gives you the crucial '**why**' of the project. If the people working on the project don't understand the reasoning behind the product they are creating then they will keep making wrong turns and bad decisions. Understanding why you are building this project – for everyone involved – will mean you have a product that is focused on the most important aspects and achieving a happy client.

Another example: we worked with a pharmaceutical brand to produce a VR experience that promoted a medical treatment for eyes. The fact that this treatment helped reduce eye degeneration with age – and in some cases even improved eyesight – made the visual clarity of the product hugely important. As a 360 video product this strongly affected the scenes we chose to shoot, the cameras we used, the way we lighted and so much more, right through into app production.

Here are a few more examples and the problems they solved:

Visualise – Médecins Sans Frontières (MSF, aka Doctors Without Borders) – Forced from Home[1]

Problem: people do not understand what it is really like in refugee camps in war-torn areas and the struggles patients have gone through to arrive where they are. They do not understand the scale of the problem and the work that MSF does internationally.

Solution: telling the story of the doctors and the patients, using VR films, allows MSF to transport potential donators into the refugee camps, into the homes of and wards of patients and doctors alike. This greatly increases the understanding and empathy towards the work of MSF. Ultimately the target is donations.

Imagination and Rewind – Jaguar I-Pace launch[2]

Problem: there was only one prototype car and Jaguar was announcing a revolutionary move into electric, competing with Tesla. They had to show the car to as many journalists as possible in the most compelling way possible.

Solution: launch the car in VR in multiple countries from the Los Angeles autoshow. Use VR to allow people to explore the unique design and layout of this fully electric car.

Adam&Eve, Outsider and Visualise – Waitrose[3]

Problem: Waitrose had a TV campaign that highlighted their organic and responsible farming; the campaign was showing views of farms that highlighted this. However, how could they convince people that these were real farms and not constructs for TV?

Solution: shooting the TV advert at the same time and at the same place with a 360 video camera allows the viewers to turn the camera themselves and explore the scene, understanding the honesty of the campaign. This meant Waitrose could take their campaign to a whole extra level of authenticity, essentially saying 'have a look for yourself'.

The above examples have very specific needs they are addressing. Sometimes, however, the brand/client just wants to get noticed against their competitors. Take for example the Goodwood Festival of Speed, one of the world's top motorsport events. There, manufacturers show their most exciting new cars and prototypes, thrashing them up the Goodwood hill climb. The manufacturers are often looking for ways to pull customers to their stands, show them something memorable and engender brand loyalty.

When such opportunities arise and the business case is less clear cut, then you know that you have to produce an experience that is going to blow people's socks off and make them talk. This can be the 'why' – to make a splash and generate buzz.

Who *do you want to see this?*

Clients and brands usually have a very specific target market for a given product. It is important to identify early who these people are, as it can inform choices on the type of experience being made. For example, a promotional VR film for a sports fashion brand like adidas by Stella McCartney will have a totally different target market to the MSF and their refugee empathy piece. The 'who' target market is intrinsically linked to the 'how' they are going to be reached, and deeply affects the type of VR that is going to be produced and the way it is made.

'Who' does not simply just mean demographics, but can also explain their profession. Looking again at the I-Pace example, the 'who' was:

- motoring journalists;
- tech journalists;
- celebrities/influencers.

These three areas were very carefully chosen to achieve the maximum impact with the launch and increase the amount the car was talked about. Doing this project only for the automotive press would not have seen nearly the impact of bringing in the wider tech press and, of course, celebrities and influencers.

What *do you want people to* see, feel *and* do?

This is where the creative sits. Now that you know what the problem is, and who it is addressed to, you can think about what you want people to see, feel and do. We find this is a great exercise to go through with a client quite early on, as they often have a very clear idea of one – if not all – of see, feel and do.

With 'see', let's go back to our Audi TTRS example – in the simplest form, they wanted people to see the new TTRS, learn about it and ideally drive it. They wanted people to 'feel' excited, amazed and inspired. Finally, for the 'do', they wanted people to register an interest to buy the car.

You could easily jump in at this point, get a test driver to drive the car and film it from the car and from the exterior as it passes, etc. However, a good VR experience – that really hooks people in and gets them more deeply aligned with the brand – needs a story. In this case Audi chose design.

Audi have a number of internal brand ambassadors and one of these was Jürgen Löffler, the senior exterior designer of their cars. He had been at the heart of the redesign of one of the most iconic Audi's of all time – the TT. So we planned that Mr Löffler would introduce us to the car at the Audi test track, explain the design process and how the new TT ended up looking like this, with particular attention to the extra styling tweaks on the RS. Then he would take us on a drive explaining the link between the styling of the TT and its power/muscle.

The latter part of this experience was meant to be a thrill, with Mr Löffler speeding the car around the track and generally putting a smile on everyone's face. We were not to know (and neither was Audi apparently) that their senior exterior designer was actually a very timid driver! That, coupled with the fact that the car was a prototype, meant he was doubly scared of damaging it. Still, the experience looked fantastic and people got a great look and feel for the car, albeit at a more leisurely pace than we might have wanted!

Looking more deeply at 'feel' you can see this quite broadly too; do you want someone to feel like they have learnt more about your company or to feel surprised by something they have learnt, or to feel shocked and amazed? The recent remake of Stephen King's *IT* has had a cinematic VR trailer made[4] – this is a brilliant use of VR for marketing. They are giving fans the opportunity to be in the world of the film, actually be in the scenes and be terrified by the notorious clown Pennywise. So in this case, they want people to feel scared! They want people to watch the film in their Google Cardboard or on their computers or phones and be so frightened that they scream out loud at their desks! This behaviour ultimately leads to what people then do.

Do you want people to buy a holiday after watching a virtual one? Buy a car after their virtual test drive? Tell their friends about the film they have just seen a 360 trailer for? Share their experience with others? Ask a customer service attendant for more information? What is it that you want the user to do?

Ultimately the 'do' part of any VR campaign should be closely linked to the KPIs, that is the resulting outcome of what they have just experienced. It is your responsibility at this stage to make it as easy as possible for people to share the experience. If it is a physical activation then ensure that the person can have something afterwards that is easy to share, whether or not that means a personalized link to the experience they have just had or a photo of them in the experience. Make sure there are very clear calls to action.

How *do you want people to see this?*

This is the major constraint in VR: how people actually consume the content. The 360 trailer for the 2017 film *IT* is a great example. I can watch it relatively comfortably on my laptop, clicking and dragging the footage around; I may pass it on to a friend, I may not. However, when you try it in a headset, I challenge you not to scream out loud and be compelled to pass it to a friend/colleague. The difference in impact and quality of experience on the different platforms associated with VR is massive.

In an ideal world we would all have VR headsets and use them regularly, meaning great VR content could be shared as much as it would justify. But this is not the case, so as a marketer you need to be very clued up as to how to distribute VR content.

The *New York Times* was one of the first companies to really confront this; they saw the potential in VR long before their competitors and started producing 360 content.[5] They knew there was a lack of headsets out there, so they partnered with General Electric in 2016 and mailed out 5 million Google Cardboard headsets to all of their print subscribers all over the United States; they have since followed up with 300,000 more to all of their digital-only subscribers.

This is obviously an extreme case but it shows how a brand was able to ensure the content they were producing was seen in its best light (or as close to best light as possible!). On smaller scales Google Cardboard has been enabling brands to democratize VR and reach large numbers of people. The headsets can be folded up and flat packed, they can be branded, printed on, made out of cardboard, foam, plastic, whatever you want.

If the desire is for the experience to allow people to communicate live with each other, over different continents, while also seeing an interactive, explorable version of the car in front of them, with room-scale tracking, as with the Jaguar I-Pace, then there is realistically only one or two platforms this could ever be delivered on – the HTC Vive or the Oculus Rift.

Often with VR campaigns, there is an understanding that there is a limited initial number of people who can see a 'premium' version of the experience. This might be at a conference, trade fair, public activations at train stations, shopping malls, etc. Then there is an online version made – for posting to 360 social channels such as YouTube or Facebook.

It may also be that the focus of the campaign, from the off, is for online usage, with VR headsets being a bonus. This was the case with one of our bigger projects – Re-Rendezvous with Ford Mustang (2016). This incredibly ambitious project looked to re-create the opening scene from a cult driving film of the 1970s, *Rendezvous*. In the opening scene, a Ferrari is driven at breakneck speed through the streets of Paris, racing to meet the 'rendezvous'; an embrace with a lover at the top of the steps to the Sacre Coeur.[6]

Of course, the beauty of shooting this scene in 360 degrees was that at any time you can turn the camera around and see the nose of the Mustang bearing down on you. Crucially, as we knew this was for online usage primarily, and not for headset, the footage could be shot from a more dynamic angle and left to be raw and bumpy, to match the original footage. It also meant that we could leave turns in the footage and not just rely on the straights as we may have had to if this was primarily for VR headsets.

A view like the one achieved, with nothing to ground the viewer when their whole world turns as the car turns a corner, would be quite uncomfortable on a VR headset. If we were to produce this project primarily for VR we would heavily stabilize the footage and have to make edits that drastically change the creative outcome of the project. So knowing how you are expecting people to view the footage directly influences what you make and how you make it.

Vision

Once the above is established you can create a vision for the project. The vision should be an idealistic view on the outcome of the project. It is an aspirational description of what you want to achieve at the end of the project, it is where you want to go. It is intended to serve as a clear guide for directing decisions throughout the course of the work, for example:

adidas: to create a VR experience that pulls people into the world of adidas classics, making them feel a part of the culture of each item. They should really feel like they are on the streets in each era and part of some incredible moments in time. Ultimately this inspires them to buy the shoes and evangelize the range.

Virgin Trains recruitment: to transport people along the width and breadth of the Virgin Trains lines, showing the beauty of the landscapes and the variety of roles involved in keeping this complex and diverse company going. Ultimately leading to a better understanding of Virgin Trains and more recruitment applications for roles outside of 'train driver'!

A vision of the project should be shared by all stakeholders and should be clearly stated in any statements of works regarding production. It should be something you always have in the back of your mind throughout production.

The reality of production

The above rules/processes look very black and white but, in reality of course, things are often shades of grey. You may have a client who wants to do a VR activation because their marketing director has seen a competitor doing it and does not want to be left behind. In this case you will need to reverse engineer the above list, but you should still try to establish the why, who what and how and write them down and share them with the team. Or, you may just be very short on time and have to move faster than some of the above allows. In this case, understanding the importance of the above foundations and principles will help you to deliver a successful project.

Key performance indicators (KPIs)

KPIs are agreed markers of a project's success. The famous question – 'How do you measure success?' KPIs are what you measure against once the project has finished or reached an agreed period. It is good to establish these early, as knowing that there are some solid figures you are aiming for can help focus the project. It also informs what is produced and potentially avoids producing features that have little or no effect on the KPIs.

Some examples of KPIs we have used in VR projects include:

- number of downloads of a VR app;
- number of views of a 360 video on Facebook or YouTube;
- number of likes or shares on social media;
- dwell times;
- bounce rates;
- holidays sold (benchmarked against not using VR);
- increase in number of recruits when using VR (or decrease!);
- amount of press generated – blog posts, newspapers, etc;
- increased number of sales.

Developing the creative

This is where good directors really earn their crust. Taking a client's brief, understanding the why, who, what and how and then distilling all that into a story/experience that flows and ticks all the boxes is a huge challenge.

At this stage the creative can be shared as a 'deck', the broad ideas for each part of the story laid out, with mood boards and annotations to explain their thinking. This deck allows for a back and forth with the client, before the production of a storyboard. One of the main challenges for the creative at this point is balancing ambition with the realities of time and budget.

The deck layout should cover the following:

- Inspiring/eye-catching first page.
- Production company or agency credentials.
- Vision of the project (as discussed earlier in the chapter).
- Director's approach – here the director can lay out the main story beats against accompanying pages of reference images/mood boards.
- Production approach – the broad plan and parts involved in the production.
- Production workflow – explain the steps that will be taken from pre-production, through to delivery.
- Technical considerations – camera choices, 360 audio considerations, if interactive then app build choices (eg Unity or Unreal), hardware choices for delivery, etc.
- Relevant case studies.
- Contact details.

Statement of work (SOW)

Once the broad creative and pricing is agreed a statement of work (SOW) should be drawn up and agreed. SOWs are vital for both the client and the content creator, as they ensure alignment on all aspects of the project and reduce any ambiguity. In short, an SOW should contain the following:

- Practical details of who each party is (company numbers, addresses, etc).
- Written confirmation of agreement of project commencement (literally just formalizing previous e-mails or calls greenlighting the project).
- Description of the work involved in the project.
- Vision of the project.
- Creative overview.
- Agreed product features.
- Services provided.
- Deliverables.
- Fees and milestones (including shoot/development dates).
- Term (length of project).
- Terms and conditions of service (content creator).
- Contact details.

The more time spent building and agreeing the SOW between the client and content creator then the better the understanding between all involved and the smoother the outcome of the project. Sometimes we arrange a half-day with clients, who come to the studio and work through it with us, meet the team and chat it all through.

Benjamin Franklin once said, 'by failing to prepare you are preparing to fail' – never a truer word said when it comes to VR projects!

Storyboarding for VR

Once the project is signed off, the more detailed stage of storyboarding can begin. Storyboarding happens on 50 per cent of projects in reality, but it is hugely helpful to have them and reference them both on shoot and in post-production. Storyboarding is also a very useful tool in interactive VR production, and does not need to be tied to linear narratives. A good storyboard is drawn up with the director and a storyboard artist; it shows the key parts of the story and explains the action. It is a visual representation of what will be captured on a VR shoot and reduces any ambiguity on the production day. Figures 4.1, 4.2 and 4.3 show some example images taken from a VR storyboard from one of our projects with Oakley.

Figure 4.1   Oakley Prizm storyboard

SOURCE Visualise (2015)

Figure 4.2   Oakley Prizm storyboard

SOURCE Visualise (2015)

Figure 4.3   Oakley Prizm storyboard

SOURCE Visualise (2015)

People often make VR storyboards with a wider perspective – showing a bigger field of view, more of a letterbox shape. This can work particularly well if there is a lot of information in the scene that is important to show. Other than this, storyboarding in VR is no different to storyboarding in other mediums.

The importance of comfort in VR

Before we move into production itself, a key term in the VR vocabulary, 'comfort', relates to how comfortable people feel in an experience. VR is such a powerful and intense medium that when executed poorly, or badly thought through, can make people feel physically ill. Get it wrong or follow poor advice and potential customers will be associating your brand with feeling seasick! Why is this? Well it comes down to the dislocation between what you see and what you feel. Your body is constantly feeding back to you from the physical environment; if you stand up, there are considerable forces of acceleration and deceleration on your inner ear that perfectly line up with the world you see changing perspective around you.

Let's take the simple example of getting out of a car, the kind of scene we are often asked to produce. If you were to film this on a 360 camera – the point of view of someone first turning and then standing up and moving sideways out of the car – then when watching this back you would see your perspective change but not feel it. You would not feel you had control over this movement too – and this combination would leave you feeling queasy. You would see the view rotate in front of your eyes but you have not turned your head, you would be pulled sideways out of the car and you would rise up all in one smooth motion. You will feel awful.

If this car example was in a real-time, game engine, then it would work well. You would be able to pull a lever or push a button on the door, it would open, you would then be able to stand up and get out of the seat as you would in the real world – of course, if the real car was not also in the real world you may find yourself grasping for support from a car that does not exist!

Comfort is also affected by technical aspects such as how quickly the headset responds to the movement of the user's head. On cheaper headsets like the Google Cardboard, especially when using older phones to drive the experiences, there can be a lag between what you see and your head moving. It may be fine for the first 15 seconds or so but will get progressively more uncomfortable the longer you keep using it. Low frame rates from machines/phones that are struggling to run the content can also lead to discomfort. One of the big challenges in VR marketing is how you achieve the creative objectives, whilst also keeping the experience comfortable.

360 video production

With the SOW, vision and storyboard all in place then pre-production can kick off. This could be looking into locations, booking studios, equipment, test shoots, etc. At this stage, a 360 video project is not hugely different to a video shoot, as long as the producer is bearing in mind the upcoming aspects of location and equipment and how they will affect the shoot day itself.

Key points

Before you move forward I want to explain some of the terms I am going to speak about below, everyday lingo in 360 video.

Stitching

The process of blending videos shot from a 360 video camera. The camera typically has between two and six lenses, each recording their own videos. These videos all need to be aligned, overlapping each other, and then carefully blended together so that the intersection between videos becomes invisible and the stitch 'seamless'. This is not always possible, but is becoming far more possible as the technology is developing!

Optical flow

A method of stitching that does not just apply a best-guess template to aligning videos on a seam, but rather looks at the objects in the scene and tries to manipulate the images to match. Nine times out of ten this leaves a seamless stitch, sometimes it looks a lot worse! Optical flow was purely for high-end and expensive platforms like the Foundry's Cara VR, but new entrants to the market, such as SGO's Mistika, have democratized optical flow stitching.

Algorithmic stitching

Camera's like Google's Jump and the Jaunt One are designed to be stitched on the cloud, ie you upload the content to Google or Jaunt and they send you back stitched footage at a later time. This stitching is based on a series of ever-evolved algorithms that match the number of cameras and their specific orientation. It is fairly good most of the time, but when it comes back with issues then you have got quite a painful process of trying to make a better job out of the 16 odd cameras of footage!

3D 360

360 videos can either be shot in 'mono' or in 3D. Shooting in 3D allows you to see a sense of depth in the scenes, giving a feeling like you can reach out and touch things around you. It is more complicated to capture and post-produce, though.

Zenith

The top of a sphere – therefore, what you see when you look up in a 360 video.

Nadir

The bottom of a sphere – therefore, what you see when you look down in a 360 video.

Equirectangular

This is the name given to the shape of a 360 video. Rather than a traditional 16×9 (wide screen) or 4:3 ratio of normal film, equirectangular footage is 2×1 ratio. In this form, the 360 video looks very distorted, but that distortion disappears when we project the video in a headset or online in a 360 video player.

The shoot

For the actual shoot day/days, if you have a well-planned storyboard and script then the production should run very much like any traditional film shoot – you will have most of the same crew, from the camera assistant, right through to the director, and require the usual belts and braces of call sheets and tightly run productions. There are a number of unique considerations though, including: specialist VR directors, VR supervisors, specialist directors of photography (DOPs), specialist digital imaging technicians (DITs), specialist technicians, ambisonic or binaural audio capture, set builds in 360, on set reviews/direction, acting/actors and moving the camera, each of which I will cover below.

Specialist VR directors

Directing VR is a technically complex challenge. You have to think about the scene in a very different way to how normal 16×9 films are shot. There is no specific composition, so you have to consistently place yourself in the position of the camera and think, what is it going to feel like from here? The actors have to think of the camera as a person, a head. Next, a good VR director needs to understand the greater flow of the story, where their user is likely to be looking, how to ensure they are looking where you want them to at a specific moment and how one scene will flow naturally into the next scene.

Often, at Visualise, we work with very talented, traditional, directors and we have to give them the technical VR knowhow to complement their creative skills and help the project reach its aims. This role we call VR supervisor.

Specialist DOPs

Lighting for 360 shoots is very hard, as there needs to be a deep understanding of where the lights are to be hidden, and if not hidden, how they will be removed in post-production. So again, the DOP will need to work closely with the VR supervisor and/or VFX supervisor to understand the best trade-off for lighting a scene beautifully but still falling inside the post-production budget.

If there is a danger for people to say 'we'll fix it in post' on traditional productions, this is far more tempting in VR, where the camera sees everything. You have to be careful though, as the post pipeline is already quite long in VR!

Specialist DITs and technicians

Handling data and cameras on a VR shoot is very different to traditional cameras. Take the Yi Halo, for example, this camera has 17 individual memory cards! One for each of its camera modules. These need to be carefully removed and batched with Google Jump software, which is a time-consuming and difficult process.

VR cameras have a lot of quirks and issues. In Chapter 5 you will hear all about the different options in greater detail, but for now, suffice it to say that you need someone on set with a lot of experience in running the camera of your choice – they need to know where the stitching lines will be, the dead spots of no content, the time it can run before overheating and many more unique issues.

Ambisonic or binaural audio capture

If you are capturing video in 360 you should be capturing audio in 360 too. This is a very specialist field that requires specialist knowledge and equipment. There are a number of 360 microphones in the market now, but we have always favoured the Ambeo by Sennheiser, and we actually worked very closely with them on its development. Whilst an ambisonic microphone can capture an ambience of a scene in 360 it still needs to be augmented with high-quality microphones aimed at or placed on key subjects and parts of the scene. Each of these tracks are then built in to full ambisonics and binaural in post, allowing the headset to track the position of the user's head and have the sound match it perfectly.

Some of the best audio engines use more than just volume to help you track the position of a sound. They also use 'phase difference', which is the difference in time that a sound has to travel from one ear to the next, a key way that we determine position of sound in the real world. Arguably, audio is far further ahead in its mimicry of the real world and its precision than video is at the moment.

Set builds in 360

If you are shooting a drama or documentary, whatever it is, the camera will see everything, so finding that perfect location is a lot harder, hiding the team too is harder. One of the tricks we frequently employ is mounting a camera, such as the Yi Halo, upside down from the ceiling, with its 'top' camera pointing down. This means all of the lighting and other rigging can be hidden in the blind spot where the camera is mounted and then removed in post with a clean plate shot while the room is empty and free of rigging, from the same exact position (see Figure 4.4).

On-set reviews and direction

It is often quite a slow process getting content off a high-quality VR camera and stitching it for review and feedback on set. So, we often set up a secondary, live streaming, camera that allows clients and directors to watch on a second screen in another area. They can even watch on a VR headset, seeing as close as is possible the view of the final image. This obviously also makes directing tricky – the director is not watching the action in the flesh, so they need to use their imagination a lot to think how things are looking from the perspective of the final film (see Figure 4.5).

Figure 4.4　Shot from a Visualise project for Don't Panic Agency and the ICRC (Note the upside down camera and the lighting rig set up above it and hidden in the camera's blind spot. Also note, the Z-Cam S1, in this case, the S1 is used as a live streaming camera, so director and client can watch live in another room)

Figure 4.5　Clients and crew watching a performance behind the scenes on a live 360 preview camera; in the screen you can make out a music act in the centre and the big, main 360 rig at the bottom and back of the image. Visualise shooting for Global Radio

SOURCE　Image courtesy of James Medcraft (2018)

Acting for 360

Given cuts are less frequent in VR and scenes are often longer and shot from one camera position, actors need to remember lines and act more like the theatre than on traditional film productions. This means more time in rehearsal and also that some actors who look great in normal adverts or dramas can end up looking a little awkward in VR! We've had great success in the past working with some immersive theatre groups and actors as a result.

Moving the camera

Moving cameras in VR should be done with a good understanding of the medium and consideration of the viewer's comfort. Some movements in VR are more comfortable than others, for example, turning a sharp corner is very uncomfortable, whereas gradual acceleration or deceleration in straight lines is fine. The direction should generally be forward or backwards, rather than sideways. Bobbing motion, like that if a camera is attached to the head, is particularly bad. As such, we have worked with a number of different systems to move the camera. Here are some of our favourites:

- Dolly Systems: one of these is better than all of the others – the Motion Impossible, Mantis 360 Kit (Figure 4.6). This is without doubt the king of the 360 dollys in the market, used all over the world, it is stable, highly controllable, even programmable and repeatable and has incredible dampening and gyro-stabilization.

- Cable camera systems: simply a highly tensioned zip wire that allows the camera to move from one end of the line to another. It is great when a dolly would be dangerous or impossible due to people or natural features and bumps. Zips also allow for crossing rivers or other interesting obstacles that a dolly never could.

- Track systems, from the likes of Mark Roberts Motion Control, allow for the ultimate in precision and smoothness. However, they come at a cost – both in installation, operation and then in post-production, to remove the tracks with VFX. When done well though, and with adequate budget, the result is unrivalled (have a look at the making of Ethiad Airways VR film[7]).

Figure 4.6   The 360 Mantis Kit (with a GoPro Odyssey and a Samsung
Gear360) from Motion Impossible

SOURCE Image courtesy of Andrew Shulkind and Motion Impossible (2018)

- Handheld systems: the final option for motion is for the camera
  to be handheld. There are a couple of approaches here – gyro-
  stabilized poles for smaller rigs and full steadicams for larger rigs:
  - Gyro-stabilized poles are carbon fibre monopods with a 360
    camera on one end and a gyroscope on the opposite end. This
    acts as both a counter-balance to the camera and a stabilizer,
    by countering jogs or bumps due to its own inertia. This set-up
    allows the camera to be floating far in front of the operator,
    making them a smaller part of the scene relative to steadicam.

– Steadicams are body-mounted rigs that allow an operator to carry a heavy rig smoothly and with great dexterity. The big issue here is in proximity – the operator is usually visible and very close.

If the shoot is successful and you have all you need in the can, then you move on to post-production. I would wait on that wrap party though, there's still a long road to travel!

Post-production

Post-production of VR films is similar to traditional film production, with a few notable exceptions: stitching, stabilization, editing.

Stitching

The biggest difference is stitching. This is the combining of each of the separate camera streams from within a 360 camera to make one seamless 360 video. There are a number of pieces of software dedicated to stitching VR and they have evolved incredibly quickly over the last couple of years. These are my top four programs:

- *Autopano Video Pro (AVP), Kolor*
  Kolor were one of the first companies to establish themselves in the stitching world. They came from a background of panorama stitching with their brilliant software, Autopano Giga. In 2015 GoPro bought Kolor in a smart move that signalled their intent to move into the VR camera world.

  AVP is probably the most heavily featured software and also the easiest to get to grips with. There is a huge range of options and configurability for stitching, great tools for masking and stabilizing dynamically along a timeline, the ability to make 16×9 films from 360 footage and much more. Crucially, with AVP, you can stitch and stabilize in one program, so if we're up against it on a tight deadline we will try to work in AVP.

- *Mistika VR, SGO*
  SGO came to the VR market from a background in 3D and post-production software. Their software has really blown me away, it has the best optical flow stitching I have seen in the market.

However, their interface takes a while to get to grips with and we have also found the way the software manages files/folders for its projects very frustrating.

A number of times we have run into a really tricky stitch and have found that Mistika VR is like waving a magic wand on the footage. It is really impressive at making obvious stitch lines/errors disappear. It is also brilliant at producing 3D 360 footage, as you might expect with SGO's background in 3D; compared to like-for-like stitches with AVP we found the 3D more natural and the stitching more seamless.

Mistika has recently introduced stabilization to its set of features, which greatly improves its all-round usefulness. We typically try to stitch the same piece of content in AVP and Mistika at the start of the scene and see which is coming out best – we will then use that one for the rest of the stitch!

- *Cara VR, the Foundry*
  Definitely at the premium end but incredibly powerful is the Foundry's Cara VR, working hand in hand with their Nuke platform. We use Cara when we need to work with incredibly challenging footage or ambitious projects. If you don't already work with Nuke it is going to be an expensive and long route to get up to speed, but if you do, then it is the most powerful option.

- *Jump Assembler*
  The Jump Assembler can only be used with two cameras – the GoPro Odyssey and the Yi Halo (the Google Jump cameras). The assembler is based on the cloud and you upload directly to it from the Google Jump software on your computer (Mac only at the time of writing). There are a number of options, like the resolutions you can download, whether to have 3D or mono, whether to prioritize certain areas of the stitch due to issues and even now a 'high quality' stitch option (which I'm sure everyone will just use as default!). Once you have uploaded to Google you have to wait for it to come back, and from our experience this can be anything between 6 and 48 hours, depending on the amount of footage you push their way. At the time of writing, Google is not charging for this service, but I understand this will soon be changing.

Stabilization

Some stabilization should be applied to 360 video footage shot from moving positions, be they on helmet cams, cars, wire cam set-ups or dollies. This is primarily for reasons of comfort – shaky, unstable footage can make people feel quite ill! Stabilization must be applied to the stitched, equirectangular, footage. Both AVP and Mistika have their own stabilization, and if that is not looking good enough we jump out into SynthEyes by Andersson Technologies.

Editing

As mentioned above, 360 video is edited in its 2×1 ratio, equirectangular projection. This makes it quite hard to understand if coming from a traditional film background; items in the foreground look compressed and small, while the ceiling and floor seem stretched out of proportion. The most famous and recognizable equirectangular projection is that of the globe, shown in Figure 4.7. Whereas, a more realistic projection by actual land mass would look like that shown in Figure 4.8.

Editing software such as Adobe's Premiere have been introducing VR tools at a fast rate, meaning it is easier than ever to edit in 360 and you can easily check your work outside of the equirectangular projection. You can even edit work in a headset now, although the tools when actually in VR are still quite crude.

Figure 4.7 Equirectangular projection, as commonly used in 360 video

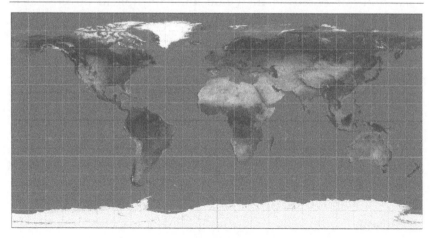

Figure 4.8 Projection of the world based on land mass, showing a more natural projection that is more representative of the areas of the film as seen in a headset

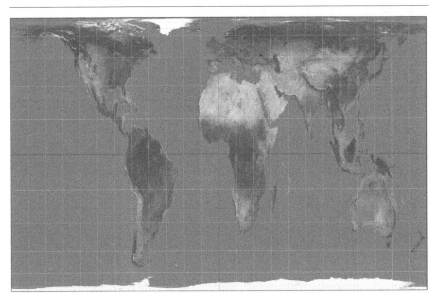

Interactive VR production

Pre-production

As mentioned earlier, the phases of pre-production for both live action VR and interactive VR share many of the same items/processes. Crucially, though, with interactive VR there should be the addition of a design document. This design document should describe how the experience will be interacted with, what the controls are, what platform/hardware is needed to use the game, etc. This can be part of the SOW (and probably should be) to ensure agreement and sign-off on all features before production commencement.

Production

Interactive VR production involves the engagement of producers, designers, artists and developers. The producers are responsible for running the project, ensuring communication between the different parties, both internally and externally to the client. The producer ensures that the production is developing in line with the design document and that the different developers, artists and designers are all supplied with the necessary assets and information in advance of each task.

Agile methodology

There are a number of management methods for interactive development but one has risen in popularity more than all the others – agile. Agile is a brilliant way of working, not just in development of interactive projects but in other aspects of production too. On some larger projects in VR film we have used agile too. Below is the agile manifesto:

Key points

We are uncovering better ways of developing software by doing it and helping others do it. Through this work we have come to value:

- *Individuals and interactions* over processes and tools.
- *Working software* over comprehensive documentation.
- *Customer collaboration* over contract negotiation.
- *Responding to change* over following a plan.

That is, while there is value in the items on the right, we value the items on the left more.

Agile is a huge topic but, in essence, this is how we interpret/use agile at Visualise on interactive projects: we work in a series of 'sprints', each a week long, which aim to cover a series of development tasks that we agree at the end of the previous week. Each day, first thing, we have a project 'stand up' – this is when everyone has to be away from their monitors and standing in a circle to discuss their progress on the sprint. This stand-up is vital for establishing issues that are blocking people in their sprints and encouraging communication between team members on ways they can help each other.

It is incredible to me how effective stand-ups are. You can have two people working next to each other on the same project, all day and they will not have discussed a potential blocker between each other until the stand-up. They were too deep in the thick of the project to see the wood from the trees. Stand-ups are perfect for giving everyone perspective on the project as a whole and the chance to think forward about the tasks ahead.

With agile, one of the main principles is iterative development and minimum viable products (MVPs). The principle is that you don't work behind closed doors, from the design document, building up the product over a long period of months, only to unveil something to the client that they don't feel aligned with/does not meet their expectations at the end (this, more traditional philosophy of production, was called waterfall). Rather, you supply your progress to the client at the end of each sprint, even in its earliest stage. Then, each week you iterate and evolve the project, with the client being a very integral part of the outcome – leading to no surprises at the end and hopefully a very happy client.

Designers

Whilst the principles of the design of the VR experience are laid down in pre-production, it is important that the designers are still involved during the production phases of the project, to ensure the user experience (UX) and user interface (UI) are developing as planned. As VR projects evolve there are often issues or constraints that arise due to the nature of pushing the boundaries of technology. At these stages we need to have reappraisals of the design.

Artists

The artists build the animations, 3D models, characters and environment for the VR experience. For example, we worked with a 3D artist when we created a virtual museum for the Van Gogh Museum and Facebook to house the five sunflower paintings. These paintings had never been in the same room before so we brought them all together for the first time in history. The room had to be designed and the frames for the paintings had to be faithfully re-created in 3D to exactly match the look of the originals. 3D artists use programs such as Maya and 3D Studio Max and will produce the 3D assets described by the designers in the design documentation. These assets will be used by the developers in building the experience.

Developers

The developers work with either Unreal or Unity, the two predominant game-engine (aka real-time engine) platforms. The beauty of both Unreal and Unity is that they allow developers to build complex experiences/games and then port them to a variety of platforms with relative ease. So if you build an experience for the Oculus Rift then with a few tweaks this can be made to work on the HTC Vive, for example.

There is an ongoing argument in the VR industry over which is the better platform for development and it seems that there are positives and negatives of both, but realistically both platforms are brilliant and certain projects may suit Unreal, others Unity. As broad strokes though, Unreal is better known for graphical fidelity, life-like lighting, etc, and Unity is better known for extreme customization capability.

In the game engine, the artist's assets are programmed and assembled. At this stage too, the developer will light and texture the scenes. This can be done hand in hand with the artists. Lighting in game engines works very much along the lines of lighting in the real world, where light sources can be placed and manoeuvred to make the scenes look their best. This technique will use more computer power in the final program, so the light is sometimes 'burnt in' to the scenes, saving processor drain but reducing the realism and dynamic nature of the scenes.

Testing

Once all of the assets have been incorporated, the scenes lit and textured and the engine programmed there needs to be a stage of testing and feedback loops. The experience will need to be optimized to work smoothly on the devices it is made for. Often smoothness can be achieved by reducing the amount of detail in the scenes. Game-engine scenes are built up of polygons, tiny triangles that fit together to make a mesh that, when seen from a great enough distance, looks organic and convincing.

In optimizing VR experiences, sacrifices often have to be made to the look and feel in order to achieve smooth running on platforms that run on smaller/less powerful processors. This is particularly true when building VR for mobile-based devices such as Google Cardboard and Samsung GearVR.

Conclusions on VR production

VR production is a complex and varied subject, covering two, largely different disciplines – VR film and interactive VR. Both forms of VR, though, follow the same principles – careful planning and scoping in pre-production to ensure successful project outcomes. There are many transferable skills from the worlds of film production and game development; however, there are large underlying differences in the techniques of telling stories and taking users on journeys, which are still being established.

It is partly this last fact, that the rules are still being written, that makes VR such an exciting space to work in. There are very few areas in the media landscape that actually allow people to break new ground. VR is one of those.

Notes

1   Médecins Sans Frontières – Forced from Home Campaign (2016) [accessed 8 April 2018] Visualise [Online] http://www.forcedfromhome.com/ and http://visualise.com/case-study/msf-doctors-without-borders-forced-home

2   Jaguar I-Pace VR Launch (2016) [accessed 8 April 2018] Imagination and rewind [Online] https://imagination.com/work/launch-jaguar-i-pace-concept

3   Waitrose 360 Video Advert (2017) [accessed 8 April 2018] AdamandEve, Outsider, Visualise [Online] http://visualise.com/case-study/waitrose-tuna-360-ad

4   Warner Bros (2017) [accessed 8 April 2018] Pictures (15 August) IT: FLOAT – a cinematic VR experience [Online] https://www.youtube.com/watch?v=FHUErvVAeIw

5 New York Times VR (2018) [accessed 8 April 2018] nytvr, *New York Times* [Online] http://www.nytimes.com/marketing/nytvr/

6 Ford Mustang on Mashable (2016) [accessed 8 April 2018] Visualise [Online] http://mashable.com/2017/02/17/re-rendezvous/#xqaHivmvV8qs

7 Ethiad Airways (2016) [accessed 8 April 2018] The making of Etihad Airways VR brand campaign [Online] https://vimeo.com/169625144

Virtual reality cameras   05

Which to use and when

One of the key differences of 360 video productions to normal productions is the cameras themselves – typically a ball of cameras that shoot in all directions. This means sets and scenes need to be managed in a completely different way. Typically crews need to hide, lights need to be more carefully considered and scenes have to work from every angle, not just 'forward'. Whilst there are ways of shooting 360 in 'plates', which means these issues are mitigated, the majority of shoots need to be considered in their 360 capacity.

When shooting 360 video, one of the first things to consider is what camera to use and when. There is no perfect 360 video camera. There is the right camera for the right job, though. Sometimes that is something simple and GoPro based, sometimes it is something complicated and high end like a Red or Arri system. There is a time and a place. Shooting 360 video is very much a game of compromises – making exchanges in quality for stitching or for being more dynamic. This is not an exhaustive list of all the cameras in the industry (there would not be enough pages in this book!) but rather are the highlights from my experience at Visualise. Here's some of my favourite cameras and when to use them.

3D cameras

First up, let's look at 3D 360 cameras. You should note here that you will only see the difference on headsets – not if you are watching the content on desktop or mobile. This is why it is often hard to justify the extra costs of shooting 3D – it gives stunning immersive results though and is the best way to produce 360 content for VR headsets.

GoPro Odyssey

The first generation 'Google Jump' camera, this is a very hard device to get hold of! We managed to wrangle one at Visualise and have since modified it to work with more practical batteries (it comes with a battery the size of a car battery), added a zenith (top) camera and the ability to remotely monitor content. We use the Odyssey when we have scenes with a lot of action around the camera that need to be in 3D. It stitches algorithmically, on the cloud, which means you don't have any 'traditional' stitch lines.

In Google's own words:

> The Jump team partners with camera manufacturers to build professional, high-quality VR cameras. Footage from those cameras runs through the Jump Assembler, which uses computer vision algorithms and the computing power of Google's data centres to create 3D 360 video. The Odyssey is the first generation Jump camera, the Yi Halo is the second generation Jump camera.

The Odyssey gives 3D 360 video of dynamic scenes but you have got to add in the top and bottom cameras manually. The camera is quite large, which means it is not suited to small areas such as car interiors, especially if you want to add on a top and bottom camera seamlessly.

Figure 5.1   GoPro Odyssey

SOURCE   Image courtesy of GoPro (2017)

Also, with people getting too close to the camera you start to see strange artefacting, where the stitching algorithms cannot work out what goes where. You also have a problem with people going into the 'dead zones', at the top or bottom of the shots, very hard to patch out. Another issue the Odyssey has is with lines/wires/fences in shot – these can all confuse the algorithms if they or the camera are moving but it seems a lot better when still.

The Jump Assembler also has a tendency to put wavy halos around moving objects in the scene, especially if their background is not moving. This is something we found particularly problematic with the footage we got back from the Falklands when shooting penguins in their natural habitat. There is a workaround but it involved a lot of heavy patching.[1] Even as I write this, another e-mail lands in my inbox from the Google Jump team – they have just built a workaround for the above described problem, letting you isolate parts of the footage that can be stitched without the algorithm and with just a pair of the cameras. This just shows you the rate of change and responsiveness of companies like Google and how fast they are working on their VR products.

The really good thing with the Jump system is how correct its 3D looks, it feels very natural, and if you play to its strengths you get some great results. It is not a simple case of uploading to Google and flinging what you get straight back up to YouTube though. If you want to get the best out of it you will still need to spend a decent amount of time in post-production.

Yi Halo

This is the second generation Google Jump camera. Building on the learnings of the first generation, Odyssey, this is a big step forward. The main advantage to the Yi Halo, over the Odyssey, is the camera on top, meaning the only area of the shot not covered is below you. The camera also feels a lot more carefully thought through – with a screen added to the side that allows you to see the health of each individual module and control all cameras easily and intuitively.

Figure 5.2   Yi Halo

SOURCE Image courtesy of Yi (2018)

There is also a handy app, for Android only, that allows you to view what four of the cameras are seeing (north, south, east, west). From this app, you can also fully control the camera. We have run the camera on a number of big 360 video shoots and have found it to be very reliable and the content it captures of a very high quality. It is also lightweight for its size, and robust, with no signs of any overheating.

There are a few issues; reviewing through WiFi is not the most reliable way to work on set. Especially, as we found, when on a busy set with a lot of conflicting WiFi signals (from a Teradeck in this case) meant we could not preview what the camera was seeing. Reviewing footage is also a long-winded process – removing 17 cards, one at a time, then uploading to a computer for a rough stitch, etc. This makes it hard work for a digital imaging technician (DIT). To get around this issue, we set up a secondary, live streaming camera (such as the Z-Cam S1), which allows us to view live 360 content on another screen that the client can review. This footage can also be saved and easily played back to allow for choices on content that is ultimately sent up to the Google Jump stitcher.

Kandao Obsidian

The Obsidian is fast becoming the 'go to' 3D 360 camera in the industry: it is very competitively priced, easy to use and quite reliable. As with the Z-Cam below, the Kandao uses a single ethernet cable to allow for remote monitoring, control and downloading of content from the camera. Thanks to the next generation of stitching software, making 'optical flow' more accessible, cameras like the Obsidian are able to make beautiful-looking 3D far more easily than before.

It is available in either 'R' or 'S' variants, focusing on resolution and speed respectively.

Johnny Five

AKA Stereo Slicer, this is probably our favourite rig. Also, the most restrictive! As you can see from Figure 5.4, it is a pair of Sony A7SII cameras that are synchronized by a custom trigger. We have also rigged the cameras to be powered from industry standard V-Locks so we are not depending on the tiny Sony batteries.

Shooting with this camera gives you great capability in low light and allows us to shoot in 'S-Log', maintaining all that beautiful detail in highlights and shadows – the long and the short of this. The

Figure 5.3 Kandao Obsidian R

SOURCE Image courtesy of Kandao (2017)

Figure 5.4 Johnny Five

SOURCE Image courtesy of Visualise (2017)

content looks beautiful after grading: the kind of quality you get from TV adverts and that we expect from regular video productions.

As the camera only covers around 140 degrees at a go, we have to shoot a number of plates or 'slices' to get the full 360 and here is the big issue with this camera system. You can only use it when you can control the scene and when the camera is in a static position. So you need to be very careful of the edges of your frame to make sure no one or thing moves through and disappears! For the right scene this technique has so many benefits, one of the biggest is being able to have your directors, lighting, director of photography, client, whoever, behind the camera – no need for remote viewing.

Check out our project with Google and the FT – *Dublin in the Dark* – to see examples of this set-up in action.[2]

Jaunt One

The Jaunt One is a hugely impressive camera. It has high levels of resolution and huge amounts of configurability. Using the Jaunt software you are able to control the minutiae of almost every setting in

Figure 5.5   Jaunt One

SOURCE Image courtesy of Jaunt (2017)

every camera individually. It did nearly break the back of some of our team though – it's the size and probably twice the weight of a very large pumpkin. A huge weight to carry around on shoots, not ideal if you want to move fast and catch things dynamically.

The camera is built from 24 individual, smaller cameras, therefore 24 card slots, therefore massively heavy on 'DIT' or on set logistics. It uses these 24 cameras in a similar way to the Google Jump system above – you upload your footage to the Jaunt cloud and then it stitches for you automatically and sends you back 3D footage. You can get it really quickly as 'offline' or in a longer period with a much finer stitch.

It is a very expensive camera, possibly the most expensive out there, at £95,000 in B&H Photo. At that price I would expect a really floorless camera, perhaps more justified a couple of years ago, when it was first made but I'm not so sure now.

On the positives, the quality of the sensors and the lenses is fantastic. I've seen footage from it that looks great, even in low light. Very good dynamic range too. What really blew me away though was the amount of control you have of the camera. You can tweak and manage everything about every individual camera and run previews, iterate settings, test again and really get the perfect-looking shot.

It is also worth noting that the modules are replaceable, so if something happens on a shoot you can easily replace the module and carry on. I would say though that this is not a camera to be used casually (and nor could you afford to!) as learning the control and getting used to it will take a significant amount of hands-on playing.

Mono cameras

A lot of shoots do not require 3D, either for budgetary reasons or because of other constraints. For example, shoots inside very small spaces such as car interiors or from drones, where the scenery is so far away that 3D is rendered useless. Also, for more extreme camera views, such as exterior car or helmet-mounted uses.

Z-Cam S1 Pro

The S1 Pro is the ultimate mono 360 video solution. It has larger lenses and sensors than other competitors and works better in low light. Also, crucially from the perspective of our director of photography, it has the ability to control the aperture manually on each camera.

The S1 Pro has only four cameras to make up the full 360 degree view, this means only four stitch seams, far better than the days of the GoPro-based, six camera rigs and the patchwork quilt of video it produced. The camera is controlled remotely from either an iPad or a laptop. This has allowed us to adjust exposure while shooting gigs, without having to come near the stage and remotely monitor from a creative perspective.

There really is so much to say about the S1 Pro, so I'm going to stick to the highlights. It has a brilliant shooting mode that allows you to get the full image circle on to the lens. Meaning each video almost completely overlaps the next-door camera – giving huge choices and flexibility in post-production. It can do live streams really effectively and reliably, out of the box, simply by connecting a single ethernet cable running to a computer that stitches the footage on the fly (with third-party software or with Z-Cam's own 'Wonderstitch' software). Part of the reason it is so good for live is because it does not overheat on constant running (a genuine issue with a lot of older VR cameras!).

The camera has good dynamic range, low-light capability and good-quality lenses and sensors. It sounds like I'm heaping a lot of praise on this camera, but trust me, it deserves it! There is apparently even a way you can use it to shoot 'quazi' 3D, although we have not tried that.

Figure 5.6   The Z-Cam S1 Pro

GoPro Fusion

I really love these little cameras. They have been a long time coming. For years we made 360 cameras from bonding together GoPros and finally they did it for us! The beauty of this camera is in its simplicity: two cameras, therefore just one 'stitch seam', light and waterproof (as we were delighted to discover!). For all head-mounted or extreme uses there is no better small 360 camera. As with any 360 camera though, it is not all positive. You will find it hard to stitch this footage in anything outside of their own proprietary software, which is fine while it works but painful when it does not.

Double camera set-ups

Thanks to the incredible Japanese lens manufacturer Entaniya, there is a huge range of possibilities for capturing content with just two cameras and lenses. Shown in Figure 5.8 are two of their 250-degree lenses attached to a pair of Red Helium 8K cameras. The lenses will

Figure 5.7   GoPro Fusion

SOURCE Image courtesy of GoPro (2018)

Figure 5.8 Red 'Side by Side' rig

SOURCE Image courtesy of Entaniya (2018)

also fit on the Sony A7 series and the Panasonic GH5s, giving a range of options for a range of conditions.

The main issue with a set-up like this is the large potential 'parallax' error from the camera sensors and lenses being so far apart. If you are in a tight area then this will be very apparent – so you either need to be able to carefully patch the seam or really muscle it through post-production. If you manage this though, you are using cameras with huge dynamic range and control and will be able to achieve beautiful-looking pictures.

Double set-ups also work for smaller cameras. Entaniya have a range of lenses that work for a range of cameras including GoPros. We have used a number of custom GoPro rigs over the years that use these lenses, sometimes as doubles or sometimes to give a wider field of view from a specific camera (eg a camera looking out of a car window without a stitch line in the middle of it).

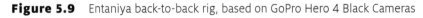

Figure 5.9 Entaniya back-to-back rig, based on GoPro Hero 4 Black Cameras

SOURCE Image courtesy of Entaniya (2018)

Single camera set-ups

Like the stereo slicer (Johnny Five) above, but just one camera, this gives perfect stitching. It can be made up from any single camera of your choice, with a very wide angle fisheye attached. We have used this set-up with the Panosonic GH5, Sony A7SII and even Alexa Mini's and Red Heliums. You simply film each 90 degrees of the full 360 view separately and then stitch them together after. You are taking every shot from the exact same point of light, called the nodal point, by rotating around the lens and not the camera body. Just as you would to do a 360 panoramic still.

Of course, you need to heavily control the scene to make sure no one moves into or out of frame but the results are fantastic, even in the smallest of spaces. We used this technique for the interior of the car on our Tempel project,[3] and for the small interior space of a passenger seat view on our Norwegian Airlines project.[4]

This set-up will give you the ultimate in quality but at the price of how dynamic the scenes can be. As with all these rigs, it is a matter of horses for courses. The great thing with the mono slicer, though, is that you can shoot 360 by just adding a fisheye to your normal camera, a great entry point to VR.

Z-Cam S1

Z-Cam has come out the blue for me and stolen a march on the 360 video camera market. The S1 is a stunning piece of kit – lenses close together, metal case for cooling, ethernet for remote control, full synchronization. The only thing it doesn't do is 3D. This is the little brother to the S1 Pro, above, and is actually still relevant for smaller, enclosed areas, as the lenses are closer together, giving an easier stitch.

Figure 5.10   Z-Cam S1

SOURCE Image courtesy of Z-Cam (2018)

We also use this as a live preview rig, allowing us to have a 360 feed direct to a headset or big screen in another room. The main rig could be something bigger such as a Yi Halo, and remain untouched for longer as creative choices can be made from the preview cam.

Other VR rigs

This section of the book is meant to highlight our favourite 360 video cameras and those that we use day in day out. It is by no means an exhaustive list of all the cameras – I wouldn't even know where to start! There are a few others not mentioned here that I would really like to get my hands on for a test.

Z-Cam V1 Pro

This is the most tantalizing of all the new 360 video cameras – it shoots 3D 360, with high-quality lenses and sensors. Combined with the right NVidia graphics card set up it can even stitch live with optical flow! Basically meaning you can get stunning-quality live footage out of it! Close lens positions, high-quality lenses and sensors, this could be the ultimate set-up.

Facebook's Surround 360 camera

Announced early in 2017, Facebook's Surround 360 camera is not your normal 360 camera. It does not just film in 360 but also captures depth information of the scene. What this means is something called 'volumetric' capture, which is often seen as the natural evolution for 360 video. The idea is that you capture a whole area to show a scene from any angle, rather than just one point. It has got a long way to go until we get to that point but cameras like the Surround 360 will be the first steps on the way.

Figure 5.11   Z-Cam V1 Pro

SOURCE   Image courtesy of Z-Cam (2018)

Notes

1   *Walk With Penguins* (2017) [accessed 8 April 2018] Visualise [Online] http://www.birdlife.org/worldwide/news/walk-penguins-ground-breaking-virtual-reality-video and http://visualise.com/case-study/walk-with-penguins

2   *Dublin in the Dark* – Google and FT (2016) [accessed 8 April 2018] Visualise [Online] https://hiddencities.ft.com/dublin/dublin-in-the-dark-the-story-of-emerald-noir

3   Tempel – ZDF (2016) [accessed 8 April 2018] Visualise [Online] http://visualise.com/case-study/360-trailer-zdfs-tv-series-tempel & https://www.zdf.de/serien/tempel/videos/makingof-360-tpl-102.html

4   Norwegian Airlines – MKTG (2016) [accessed 8 April 2018] Visualise [Online] http://visualise.com/2016/12/norwegian-vr-activation

The future of VR

As you will see time and time again through the earlier chapters of this book, we are still in the very early stages of consumer adoption for VR. This means that our marketing efforts are planned around either premium physical activations, 'we'll bring the VR to them' or higher-volume postage or handing out of Google Cardboard headsets in order to reach the targeted markets. This is a problem now, but it won't be an issue in the future.

In this chapter I will show you how VR is going to reach mass adoption, and talk about the incredible world that VR will open up for marketers in the future. First though, I was lucky enough to talk to Rohan Silva, former UK government adviser, pioneer of London's 'Tech City', BBC documentarian on artificial intelligence and founder of the Second Home workspace.

A futurist's thoughts on VR – Rohan Silva

INTERVIEW

Stuart: Thank you for joining me Rohan. Can you let us know a bit about your background?

Silva: I spent my career working in public policy in the government and the treasury and in parliament at number 10. When I was working in opposition with David Cameron, it really struck me that a lot of the time politicians think; 'we're cleverer than the people in power', so if we get in we'll do a better job. I just really think that is a very stupid way of thinking because I think we are all equally flawed. But you maybe do have a chance to do better things in government if you bring to bear new insights, new technologies and new areas of research that could structurally make government better. There are lots of examples, such as behavioural economics, etc.

Technology and digital technology is, right now, the biggest area where if governments made use of this stuff it could really make people's lives better. So that was the rabbit hole I went down and started spending more time in Silicon Valley and Israel and a lot of places to see what technologies could be transplanted into government. Also to look at how government policy might be used to support the technology industry in the UK. So that is how it all began.

Stuart: Do you think VR is an important future technology?

Silva: I think VR is likely to be incredibly important because the trend of digital over the last 50 years has been miniaturization and the disappearing, or the shrinking, of the interface between human and technology. It feels like a logical next step for this technology that sits in or around the eye and you can interact with it, in a much more intuitive way, using gesture and voice and movement. It does feel inevitable that VR is going to be a new technology platform, one way or another.

Stuart: How do you think VR can be used for marketing?

Silva: To me the wonder of VR is that it can help unlock human empathy. I think so often you hear a story or you see something happening and I think a human response is to think 'Well, that's happening in another country, on the other side of the world', or 'That particular story has no relevance to my life', 'That product or that service, that's not for me'. I think in a very deep way, VR, by bringing you closer to the action, breaks down that divide between yourself and what you are seeing and that is really moving. I think the best marketing is empathetic and it is emotional and doesn't invite you to imagine yourself enjoying or participating in the product. VR is so perfect at that.

I think the challenge is how to move from VR being a technical discipline to a creative art and that is where I think Visualise is so brilliant because you marry those disciplines. Visualise is like Apple in that you are at the intersect of arts and technology.

Stuart: How Can VR break its chicken-and-egg cycle and reach greater adoption?

Silva: It seems to me that VR is at the same stage as all great technologies pass through, which is in the hands of the technical experts. It is only just beginning to be in the hands of the creatives – that first wave of truly creative minds getting their mitts on technology that previously was in R&D labs. I personally think that using VR just to see what a product looks like or see what a table looks like in your home is not that interesting. It isn't that great a leap forward, in truth, from one-hour delivery from Amazon that you can return for free if you don't like the object. It's better but it's not to me a huge leap forward.

What is a leap forward though, and is what Visualise do so well, is storytelling around VR. That emotional connection with a product or a brand or an organization that cannot be achieved on a simple phone screen or just on TV. That I think is really exciting because it is a new avenue for storytelling and for brand connection and it is unique to the media.

Stuart: How do you think VR is going to grow in comparison with AR?

Silva: In truth I don't know. I mean they feel to me very complementary and it might be that AR is a step towards VR or vice versa. I genuinely don't know but I think it is really exciting that so much investment is going into both of these fields and it is really exciting that truly creative people are starting to play with that technology.

I think both will prosper. I think that often in the media there tends to be an assumption that something has to lose in order for something else to win. I don't think that's right. I have a feeling AR will be really well suited to some things like navigating the city and VR will be brilliant for other things like films and storytelling or sports and computer games. I think both can prosper. Again, I think the key is the creative direction and whether there is a narrative that can be told uniquely through this medium. What is the visual vocabulary that can be developed? That's the exciting bit!

Stuart: How can VR be more social?

Silva: I guess a good sign is that seeing Facebook buying Oculus, Mark Zuckerberg's public comments on VR are all centred around social. So you've got one of the five most valuable companies in the world pouring billions into VR to push it in a social direction. There is a decent bet that we will end up with quite a socialized future for VR. At a practical level, being able to put on a headset and talk to someone on the other side of the world – what that means for dating, for friendships and so on, I think it is really interesting. It feels much more social than, say, television ever did.

It is that fascinating moment where it is up to the creatives to determine the future for the technology that is there now. With the dawn of the Internet Age people predicted that what the internet would mean is that people would hide behind anonymous profiles and really stop talking to one another. Instead, what it led to was a huge explosion of personal expression through blogs, YouTube and Twitter and all the rest, which really wasn't predicted 20 years ago. The internet has become much more social and it may be that VR follows that path too – initially an individual experience but becoming more plural and social as it develops.

Stuart: How do you think VR is going to evolve?

Silva: It is a new visual medium that requires a new way of thinking. That will take time. I'm nerdily obsessed with the moment in the early 20th century when skyscrapers first started to be built. They were made possible because steel technology had developed to a point where very tall buildings could be constructed and the elevator had developed so that you didn't have to climb 30 flights of stairs.

So architects started to design skyscrapers, but of course the visual vocabulary of architecture hadn't evolved, although the underlying technology had. The first skyscrapers are covered in greek columns and have gargoyles and stone cladding, domes on top and it took another couple of decades before that was stripped away. There will be a point in VR where a new vocabulary takes over from the original.

It was the same with television; the first television programmes were radio programmes ported to television. It took years before people started exploiting the potential of the medium. Is that bridge of recovery formed yet? No. Do we know where it's going? No. But do we know that it needs to be made? Definitely.

Stuart: Is VR the future of advertising?

Silva: Whenever I talk to the advertising industry they seem to be fairly depressed right now, because a lot of the creativity in advertising has been stripped out by data targeting on Facebook and other platforms. They are sort of pushed to optimization. Maybe, and who knows, maybe VR will open up a new channel for true creativity and storytelling again in advertising. That would be a very exciting thing, and good for the industry. I think there is more to communication than a Facebook ad – it doesn't explain the centrality of a company, its values, its mission – you need other channels to do that.

If VR can actually allow companies to tell stories but in a targeted way, to demographics that are best placed to talk to, then that is really exciting. At the moment the more storytelling-centric mediums such as television advertising don't allow you to be very targeted, or magazine advertising, it doesn't allow you to really pinpoint an audience. Maybe VR could be that sweet spot between those two.

To highlight a few of Silva's thoughts on VR and its future:

- VR is an inevitable new platform paradigm for technology – it is a way of truly immersing and involving people in media.
- VR breaks down the barrier between you and what you are seeing, allowing for far stronger emotional connection and engagement with content.
- Challenge is moving VR from a technical discipline to a creative art.
- Both AR and VR will prosper; it is not a zero sum game.
- Like the internet, VR may start as an individual experience but will soon become more plural and social.
- There will be a point in VR where a new vocabulary takes over from the original, as with TV and radio.
- VR could open up a new channel for advertising that is not restricted by modern marketing trends and allows a flourishing of creative storytelling.

The route to mass adoption

VR is going to take a number of years to come to fruition and be a ubiquitous technology. The fact that people have to wear a headset is a big behavioural change that is a challenge to uptake. As a result, the drivers for people to use VR have to be very compelling. Let's have a look at what the drivers are that would get the public at large into the 'metaverse'.

Film and popular culture

With the recent release of *Ready Player One*, the movie (2018), we are seeing the beginning of a new wave of films inspired by a more immersive and virtual future, the film of the famous book by Ernest Cline, handed out to all Oculus employees as obligatory reading when they started. Directed by Steven Spielberg, this film demonstrates the huge potential of VR to the uninitiated. It is set in a dystopian future, where people escape the real world to the 'Oasis', a virtual metaverse where people play, meet, communicate and hunt for clues to a competition set up by its mysterious creator. Although a dark and often creepy film, it highlights how empowering and incredible the virtual world will be when the technology catches up with its potential.

Other films and series are also embracing a VR future – take *Altered Carbon*, the Netflix adaptation of Richard Morgan's brilliant series. They frequently jump into VR for pleasure, interrogation and, rather grimly, torture. Again the lines between the real and the virtual worlds get blurred, but again, we are educating on the potential power and uses of VR. A clever twist from a production point of view is that most of the virtual world is shot in 360 video, and displayed as an 'equirectangular' film, giving that unique distortion that we are so familiar with in VR production.

Standalone headsets

Oculus's release of the 'Go' and HTC's Vive Focus are going to massively reduce the entry barriers to VR. Both headsets allow the users to access VR without the need for a computer or a mobile phone to power the headset. In the case of the Oculus Go, this makes it considerably cheaper, with Oculus citing a price of just US $199 on launch. The Vive Focus has the extra feature of 'inside-out tracking', allowing the user to physically move around a space; this is going to push the price of these units north of $500. Crucially though, the Go is at a much more competitive price point and should lead to a lot more consumers in 2018 and beyond. As you will see from Chapter 2 on the virtual reality landscape, and our interview with Stephanie Llamas from SuperData, she sees the Go as the perfect timing to coincide with publicly accessible VR demos such as The Void, giving that spark for people to go on and buy a headset.

Windows mixed reality

I get frustrated by the name of the Windows VR platform – these are not 'mixed reality' headsets, rather they are pure VR. The sensors on the front of the headsets allow them to track the room around you, allowing you to walk around the experience, so it is volumetrically enabled VR, rather than MR. The price point of these headsets is good. They are quite competitively priced, starting around $299 and peaking at $499. Probably the most important thing about the headset though is the fact that it runs from Windows, one of the most popular operating systems in the world. This is, in a single swipe, making VR far more accessible.[1]

Six degrees of freedom

Expect more experiments in volumetric capture – capturing 'video' from an area rather than a single point. The first of these experiments will allow for a small amount of movement from the user in their body while they are watching the content, ie they can do more than just turn their head to look around themselves, they can also sway their body forward, back, left and right. Early versions of this will be just allowing a small amount of movement, perhaps six inches in any direction. Even this small amount though will greatly add to the feeling of immersion and presence.

Facebook's new volumetric cameras, from their partnership with OTOY, Adobe, the Foundry and Framestore are an exciting step forward in capturing this tricky content.[2] There are other ways of capturing volumetric content too, including using multiple camera array systems that can simultaneously film people from nearly every angle, allowing for a 3D model to be made of that person – 4D if you figure it is moving through time too! Imagine a film that you can walk around, watching the characters and scenes from different angles, and getting different insights each time you watch.

There has been a large rise in photogrammetry too, the process of capturing a 3D model of a room or place by taking hundreds or even thousands of pictures of everything in the room from any angle. There are a few software options out there, such as Agisoft's PhotoScan and Autodesk's Recap. The resulting model can then be walked around in VR, or become the basis for the real-life backdrop of a VR game or marketing activation involving interactive elements.

Another way to capture an environment immersively is with laser scanning. This typically involves the precision mapping of an area with a device that throws out missions of laser points, measuring their distances incredibly accurately. This is then melded with a 360 photo from the same position for richer colour and light information and the process is completed from numerous parts of the room. This technique produces some of the most stunning results, most famously used by the BBC in their project with ScanLabs, mapping the underground, lost cities of Italy.[3]

B2B growth

One of the key growth areas in VR in the short to medium term is going to be the business to business (B2B) sector. Already we are seeing VR being used more for training and in industries such as health care and architecture as a practical tool. The reason for this is simple – it is easier for a business to justify the currently high cost of VR than it is for a consumer. What this means for the industry as a whole though is the continued uptake and use of VR by more people. It also means the continued development of the technical aspects of VR; innovations will flow into the consumer market and, of course, into marketing and advertising.

Gaming

With the gradual growth of the number of VR headsets, we need a 'killer' game. That is, a game that everyone talks about, that makes the perfect use of the new medium and does justice to the potential of VR. Part of the issue at the moment is that the vocabulary for VR production is still being learnt, so we are still figuring out how best to make these games. But they are getting really good now! We are turning a corner, people are starting to talk more and more about these games and there will soon be enough headsets out there to start a snowball effect of increasing interest. One of the issues is that it is hard to justify the spend on a VR game from a studio's perspective as there are not enough headsets, so the VR versions are generally adaptations of existing games. This often works well, but VR is going to really sing when the games are built from the ground up for VR.

Some of my favourite titles to date include: *Farpoint* and *Wipeout VR* on the PS4; *Rick and Morty: Virtual Rick-ality* and *Robo Recall* on the Oculus Rift; *Fallout 4* and *Rec Room* on Steam.

VR films

Interestingly though, according to the Statistic Brain Research Institute (August 2017), only 48 per cent of the content viewed on headsets was games.[4] This leaves a large percentage to 360 video (aka VR films). Armando Kirwin wrote a brilliant series of articles on the health of the VR industry and mentions that the figure of 360 video viewing may be even higher:[5]

> Samsung and Google have stated that mobile headset owners are spending nearly 50 per cent of their time in headset watching video content and it may be growing. I've been told behind closed doors that gaming on mobile headsets is probably closer to 35 per cent of usage today.

People do not necessarily want to interact with content to enjoy it. In the same way that people like to sit down and watch a film, rather than play a computer game, people will sometimes want to do the same in VR. There is a time and a place for passive and interactive, they are not mutually exclusive. Soon, the vocabulary for storytelling in VR will be far more established and the number of headsets will justify more spend on film content. I think VR films, especially when you start seeing famous actors and directors in the space, are going to massively drive adoption. Hollywood is already experimenting with VR. We have seen experiments/promotional experiences for titles including *Dunkirk*, *Wired*, *Jurassic Park*, *Jungle Book* and many more. Once a film is built for VR headsets exclusively, it is only going to push adoption faster.

'VRcades'

Hugely successful already in China and growing fast in the United States, VRcades, where people pay for, or are given, a VR experience in high footfall locations are going to be a great way of onboarding new users. HTC have a licensing model for this already – expect other manufacturers to follow. VRcades allow for the ultimate possible experience of VR, with experiences being pushed to the extremes of their potential. A great example of this is 'The Void'. Standing head and shoulders against the current competition it is a window into VR of the future. Anyone who has tried The Void will understand the true potential of VR. Here is their offering in their own words:

> It's hyper-reality. It's technical achievement. But mainly, it's fun! THE VOID is a whole-body, fully immersive VR experience, full of surprises at every turn; with you, your family and friends inside the action. One second you're standing on solid ground, the next you're stepping deep into darkness, looking at unimaginable beauty – or fending off danger from another realm. Did you see it? Did you feel it? What's next? You'll just have to experience it to understand.

Also, see the link to the *Wired* review for a first-person account of The Void.[6] What it shows you is the power of combining a great franchise with cutting-edge VR technology. The clever set build and programming of the experience actually places real physical doors and buttons where you see them in the game, massively adding to the reality. Once the technology advances, we will be able to get this level of experience in the home. Until then, VRcades are going to be an important part in giving people that first taster.

Live volumetric capture

We mentioned volumetrics earlier in the chapter, when talking about six degrees of freedom, but let's take it to its natural destination – volumetric capture/scanning will be as normal in the future as filming an event. Imagine, we will be able to live stream your favourite bands, sports, events, volumetrically. So you will be able to put on your headset and walk on to Centre Court during the Wimbledon final. Watch it from perspectives far beyond the most expensive seat in the house! Or walk on stage with your favourite band, standing next to them as they perform. I think this kind of volumetric capture and playback will be one of the most important tipping points in getting the masses into VR.

Just think about how special it would be to be on the red carpet at Cannes – Clooney, Pitt, Johansson walk past, stop for photos, the photographers' flashes are firing all around you, you can stand next to them and strike a pose too, albeit in your dressing gown. What this content does is appeal to a demographic completely different to the typical tech, male, early adopter that is getting into VR now. This opens it up to anyone who is a fan of any famous event or moment.

Retail

As the market nears its tipping point we will see more retailers looking to use the unique capabilities of VR to sell products. Already, automotive marques such as Audi have been using VR to allow consumers to explore their range and even customize their cars.[7] We can expect a huge number of other industries to move into VR soon too, for one major reason – VR fills a big gap in retail at the moment, that between the high street and the home.

As mentioned in Chapter 1, experiential marketing has been a huge focus of retailers in recent years. A large reason for the success of experiential is the idea that you have to see it to believe it, or try something first hand in order to convince people. VR allows experiential in the home and I predict that by 2020 we are going to start having enough VR devices in the market for marketers to target experiential launches to this new market.

An important step for retail VR is the ease/ability to buy. Quite simply, people should be able to browse products, experience them, customize them and then buy them. This simple mechanic has not been perfected yet. People need to feel completely comfortable though and any friction in the buying process needs to be removed. Once this is done, VR will be a natural evolution of retail, transforming the way we shop and buy, and massively eroding the high street.

Social

By 2020 or 2021, I predict there will be enough people using VR regularly for communities to be established and for greater development of the mechanics of communication and interaction in VR. For social to truly work though, there does need to be a critical mass. Currently going into Facebook spaces, it is unlikely, unless you have pre-arranged a meeting, that you are going to just bump into any friends. For example, have a look at how Facebook is marketing social VR.[8]

As you will see if you read *Ready Player One*, a social environment in VR – where people can meet, communicate, play, develop themselves – is a vital part of the future of VR. Social in workplace VR is also going to be a massive area for the future – collaborations, communications and more. Ultimately, this is the creation of the 'metaverse' – another world, a virtual world that has great value to people and essentially allows us to grow VR in directions inconceivable to us now. It will allow new areas of creativity, new competitions, new employment and in turn will hugely change the real world too.

Augmented reality (AR)

If I had to choose one thing that was going to usher in VR to our futures, above all else, then I would say augmented reality (AR). There is a new surge in AR since its initial boom and bust with Google Glass in 2013 through 2015. Now, in 2018, it is being used in mobile apps, using the pass through cameras on the phones, just handheld of course. Both Apple and Samsung have announced new tools for making AR content that allows the real-world environment to be tracked; these are called AR Kit and AR Core respectively. Where things get really exciting though is when AR goes back onto the eyes.

It may seem strange that a seemingly 'competing' technology could be the key to the success of VR, but hear me out. VR will piggyback off the meteoric rise of AR. People will be wearing advanced glasses for overlaying content on the real world. These same glasses will be able to show VR content, just obscuring the real world completely in doing so. Essentially, this eliminates one of the biggest barriers to adoption – having to put a headset on – you will already have the headset.

AR is going to confer great advantage to people who wear it, love it or loathe it, and there will be a lot to loathe (watch Keiichi Matsuda's

Figure 6.1 The DigiLens EyeHud AR glasses, launched at CES 2018; Digilens are part of a raft of new companies moving into the AR space

SOURCE Image courtesy of DigiLens (2018)

horrifying Hyper-Reality[9]). But the practicalities of the medium will mean it does have the smartphone-like take-up that VR was feted to have a few years ago.

In late 2017 the long-awaited Magic Leap was finally revealed.[10] This headset follows on (and should greatly advance) the work done by Microsoft in this space on the Hololens. Right now both headsets are quite unwieldy but they allow a glimpse of a future where the real world is overlaid with information, animation, games, offers, etc. AR will get lighter and smaller and better looking to wear, ultimately to a point where it is a pair of glasses that are hardly indistinguishable from a normal pair (see Figure 6.1).

Story experiences

As the boundaries between film and interactive merge there will evolve a new kind of content. A story that you are an active part in. There are already early experiments in this area, the simplest being choose your own adventure-style experiences where people have a series of choices along the way, as the story develops. However, with volumetric capture and further development in the fidelity of game engine graphics, we will soon be experiencing worlds and stories that are in no way linear, and evolve organically around our interactions and choices. This highly complex method of storytelling will take a lot of time to develop its vocabulary but will be an incredibly strong and engaging way for people to experience content.

The Mexican film director Alejandro González Iñárritu has been pioneering this area, with an experience that lets people walk in the shoes of a Mexican migrant crossing the border to the United States (and being accosted).[11] They also can explore the area and find clothing and items left by immigrants in their crossing. Speaking on the Fondazione Prada website, Iñárritu says:

> During the past four years in which this project has been growing in my mind, I had the privilege of meeting and interviewing many Mexican and Central American refugees. Their life stories haunted me, so I invited some of them to collaborate with me in the project. My intention was to experiment with VR technology to explore the human condition in an attempt to break the dictatorship of the frame, within which things are just observed, and claim the space to allow the visitor to go through a direct experience walking in the immigrants' feet, under their skin, and into their hearts.

The experience, named 'CARNE y ARENA', has been honoured with a special award – an Oscar® statuette – by the Board of Governors of the Academy of Motion Picture Arts and Sciences on 11 November 2017. It is the first of many experiences on a path to a whole new way of telling stories and immersing and engaging viewers.

Haptics

Haptics are technologies that allow for the sense of touch – force feedback, vibration, greater movement and motion. There is already a lot of research into haptics and early products are coming to market such as the Tesla Suit,[12] Haptx gloves[13] and VRGluv.[14] However, for haptics to be refined and integrated as standard into software I think we will be looking into the future, around 2024. Haptics will be one of the big steps in making VR feel real, along with greater visual fidelity and processing power.

Visual fidelity

One of the big issues in VR uptake in the present day is the 'pixelation' of the screens in the headsets. Current high-end VR headsets such as the Oculus Rift and HTC Vive have 1080×1200 pixels per eye in resolution, which equates to around 15 pixels per degree. Humans are capable of viewing closer to 120 pixels per degree! This is an improvement of eight times the current resolutions before we don't see the pixels – or 24000×24000 pixels per eye. Obviously we are a long way off this figure, even by 2024. By this date though, we should have surpassed Michael Abrash's minimum requirements for resolution at 4000×4000 pixels per eye.[15]

Development in this area is being spearheaded by a few notable start-ups: Pimax, a Chinese start-up, boasting 3840×2160 pixels per eye and Varjo, a Finnish start-up, boasting far beyond even that. Hopefully these two start-ups show us that a next generation of visual fidelity is going to arrive sooner than 2024, but if we go by Abrash's guess, then I think the date people will stop objecting to resolution issues will be around 2024.

Metaverse

The Metaverse is the virtual world that we all operate in – ideally this is one platform, device agnostic and all encompassing. Anyone with any device can enter the metaverse and converse, explore, play, work and innovate. It is quite literally another world. How this world will look and feel is likely to be vastly different from the real world – there are no constraints of real-world physics, no laws (yet), nothing to govern how you should look or act, etc. The metaverse will likely develop to a point where it has its own currency or own way of creating value that transfers value to the real world – in much the same way that you can with games like *World of Warcraft*, where game play can result in 'gold' (the in-game currency) that can then be traded for 'tokens', which have a real-world value. With the rise of cryptocurrencies, it is likely that the metaverse will have a currency that is not attached to a particular region or country, but rather allows for value exchange on a level playing field, no matter where you are physically based.

This new virtual world will be dynamic, exciting, built on dreams of a new utopia. It will be as flawed and seedy as it is beautiful and magnificent. It will be the doorway to content, meetings, entertainment and also a draw in itself. I can't wait to go!

Mass adoption

Finally, I predict that by 2025, as a result of all the above steps, we will have mass adoption. VR will be commonplace in the home and at work. This will of course mean a totally different landscape for marketers looking to reach people through the medium – there will be critical numbers of users and headsets in the market. From a creative perspective there would be incredible potential to market in ways we cannot even begin to imagine.

Future marketing in VR

Dedicated content pieces

As with the general evolution of marketing in the age of content, a lot of the focus will be on bringing people experiences and content, with brand association. Paid-for content will usually eliminate this mechanic, as with modern-day apps/games on mobile devices. Frequently free apps are paid for by advertising revenue, and I see no reason why this would change in the metaverse. In line with the current trend towards experiential marketing, brands giving experiences, rather than just focusing on product, will be more successful.

This means that more brands will be paying for content to be produced. For example, a film that transports you back to the heyday of the mods and rockers by Dr Martens – it can have a great story, great actors and a great director. It is Dr Martens by association, not overtly. Think of the brilliant Wes Anderson short film 'Come Together' – this was paid for by H&M and they got brilliant press for it.[16]

Integrated 'out of home' marketing

The development of the metaverse will open the door to more traditional advertising, only now it will be with a new and innovative twist. As you explore the metaverse, advertisers will try to reach you, much as they do in the real world, catching your eye with stunning content. This time though, there are no boundaries, so will the road crack in front of you and a Land Rover Discovery drive out of the crevice?! Or will Usain Bolt run up to you and challenge you to a race for a pair of Pumas? In the same way that augmented reality will make anything or any place around us a potential screen or position for advertising, so will any place in the metaverse. How much we let this happen or how much we control our environments in the VR space will undoubtedly depend on who is responsible for funding it.

Targeted marketing

The nature of the metaverse being entirely digital means that data could be tracked to a far larger extent than in the real world, bringing the possibility of far more targeted adverts, based on exact metrics of people's habits rather than guesses. Imagine combining the best of the technology developed by Google and Facebook to the real world, allowing brands to target people at moments of their real lives just when they need products or services most. Of course all of this will depend on the rules of the people who create the metaverse – will they want or allow advertising in there? In its current form, perhaps not.

There will be new businesses entirely founded on the metaverse, which have no presence in the real world. For example, imagine a part of the metaverse you can go to that puts you in deep-space exploration simulation. You pay for a different adventure and every time can influence the outcome of your own story. It's like *Westworld* on steroids, with no boundaries. It is pure escapism and will be massively popular, a huge industry.

Influencers

Ernest Cline's novel, *Ready Player One*, is essential reading for anyone looking to get into VR. He imagines a metaverse where people can 'upgrade' or develop their virtual character, adding abilities and powers far beyond anything possible under the constraints of reality. From a marketing perspective this will mean the growth of a new kind of influencer – people will have their own heroes of this metaverse that they want to follow, learn from, etc. They will become a valuable commodity to advertisers looking to gain credibility and traction in this new world. Some people in the metaverse will have as much or more influence on the public at large as any of the current-day influencers.

Conclusion

When thinking about the possibilities of marketing in VR, in the future we can expect to experience the virtual world far more viscerally and intensely than is currently possible. This will lead to more shareable and talked-about content that has huge emotional impact and influence. In short, a dream for advertisers and marketers alike. But one thing I find really exciting is that we can already reach for the stars in VR production, we can already make the experiences of our heart's desires. Sure, the resolution might not be quite there and the sense of touch or smell or physical feedback not developed... but we can still land on the moon or fly a dragon, or have a face-to-face performance from Madonna or Kanye West.

The main technical blockers to VR being a success have been removed, and the industry is rolling now and picking up speed. Marketers and brands can create anything they can imagine, transport people to life-changing experiences. It is just a matter of imagination – it's the perfect time for the best creative minds to start creating something magic, and brands, you can facilitate that. What an exciting time in the real/virtual world.

Notes

1 Windows Mixed Reality Home Page (2018) [accessed 8 April 2018] [Online] https://www.microsoft.com/en-gb/windows/windows-mixed-reality

2 Hamilton, I (2017) [accessed 8 April 2018] UploadVR (19 April) F8 2017: Facebook and OTOY's volumetric camera system will deliver six degrees of freedom in 2017 [Online] https://uploadvr.com/facebook-otoy-volumetric-camera/

3 ScanLab Projects (2017) [accessed 8 April 2018] Italy's Invisible Cities, BBC One [Online] https://scanlabprojects.co.uk/work/italys-invisible-cities/

4 Statistic Brain (11 August 2017) [accessed 8 April 2018] VR virtual reality technology statistics [Online] https://www.statisticbrain.com/vr-virtual-reality-technology-statistics/

5 Kirwin, A (8 May 2017) [accessed 8 April 2018] Why 360 film is in the midst of a reboot – Part 3: Demand [Online] https://www.roadtovr.com/why-the-360-film-industry-is-in-the-midst-of-a-reboot-part-3-demand/

6 White, J (December 2017) [accessed 8 April 2018] I was a stormtrooper for 15 minutes and it was awesome, *Wired* [Online] http://www.wired.co.uk/article/star-wars-vr-london-secrets-of-empire-void-experience

7 ZeroLight Automotive VR (January 2016) [accessed 8 April 2018] Audi walking VR [Online] https://zerolight.com/projects/audi/audi-walking-vr

8 Facebook Spaces Weblink and Video (2018) [accessed 8 April 2018] [Online] https://www.oculus.com/experiences/rift/1036793313023466/

9 Matsuda, K (2016) [accessed 8 April 2018] Hyper-reality [Online] https://vimeo.com/166807261

10 Magic Leap AR (2018) [accessed 8 April 2018] [Online] https://www.magicleap.com/

11 Fondazione Prada (2018) [accessed 8 April 2018] Alejandro G Iñárritu: CARNE Y ARENA [Online] http://www.fondazioneprada.org/project/carne-y-arena/?lang=en

12 Tesla Suit Website (2018) [accessed 8 April 2018] [Online] https://teslasuit.io/

13 Haptx Gloves Website (2018) [accessed 8 April 2018] [Online] https://haptx.com/

14 VRGluv Website (2018) [accessed 8 April 2018] [Online] https://vrgluv.com/

15   Abrash, M (16 October 2016) [accessed 8 April 2018] Oculus
      Connect 3 opening keynote: Michael Abrash, Oculus [Online] https://
      www.youtube.com/watch?v=AtyE5qOB4gw

16   Essential Homme (2018) [accessed 8 April 2018] 'Come Together' – A
      H&M Holiday short film directed by Wes Anderson [Online] https://
      www.youtube.com/watch?v=aXLO2dFfwLE&t=10s

APPENDIX
Implementing your virtual reality production framework

This appendix is a form that I use on projects to better understand the brief, establish firm foundations and understandings, and track a project from inception to delivery. It draws from the principles established in Chapter 4 (Virtual reality production).

1 What is the business problem we are solving?

```



```

This could be as simple as we are not getting enough online engagement, or more specific such as our car will not be ready in time for XYZ motorshow, so we want a virtual version.

2 Who are we targeting?

```



```

A certain demographic such as students, looking for work at a grad fair, or customers of another brand, etc.

3 What do you want people to see, feel and do?

See	Feel	Do

Keep it simple here; it should be something clear that you can refer to at a later stage to remind yourself when you are in the thick of a project, eg *See* great detail of the interior of the car while in a driving experience. *Feel* impressed with the detail, invigorated by the experience. *Do* – tell their friends about it, share it, enquire more about the car.

4 How do you want people to see this?

Is this for online or headset? If headset, which one? Is there a secondary or tertiary deliverable such as a projection dome?

5 What are the project KPIs?

It is always good to have key performance indicators (KPIs) established on a project, as not only does it allow you to prove success it also gives great confidence to the client that you are willing to be judged by them. As you will know though, from Chapter 1's dive into return on investment (ROI), there are a lot of ways that VR performs very strongly when compared to other mediums. These KPIs can be related to the specific business problem, eg a project with us for Virgin Trains recruitment had a KPI that indicated the increased/decreased number of recruitment applications on a student fair compared to the same stand the previous year.

6 What is the vision for the project?

```
[                                                                    ]
```

This is an idealistic view on the outcome of the project, eg by showing customers our VR experience, we want them to understand the possibilities and benefits of using our product more.

At this stage, the document can dive in to a lot more detail and can essentially stand as a statement of works (SOW). The beauty of using this as a statement of work is that it has all of the above foundations of deep project understandings before the more descriptive and practical parts of an SOW. The first part can be completed in the early stages of pre-production or pitching and the below in the mid to latter stages of pre-production.

7 Creative overview of the project:

```
[                                                                    ]
```

More descriptive and in depth than the vision, lay out how the project will meet the vision.

7 What is the project timeline?

Stage	Date
Pre-Production:	
Production:	
(Post-Production) 360 Video Only	
App Production	
Quality Assurance (QA) Testing	

As a general rule, for 360 videos, we try to have 50 per cent of the time in pre-production that we do in post-production. A typical project for us would have two weeks' pre-production, a three-day shoot, four weeks' post-production, which runs parallel with app production. The final step is of course QA testing, which you must allow another one or two weeks for as there are always snags/unforeseen changes needed in VR projects. Unless you are very lucky, you should plan for it.

8 What are the project fees and milestones?

We usually ask for 30 per cent or 50 per cent of the project fee upfront, depending on the nature of the business. With a lot of 360 video projects there are locations, fixers, casting agents, directors, etc to pay at the start of projects. Then we stage later payments on post-production commencement and project completion. With interactive development too, it is good to stage milestones and payment in advance, which helps to avoid 'creep' where features and requirements are gradually added that were not originally part of the scope.

9 Description of works:

This is a really key section to discuss and share with the client. It is very important to agree scope and boundaries, and to be as specific as possible here. For example, creative development of initial ideas, scriptwriting, storyboarding, location sourcing, casting, 3D 360 video capture, ambisonic audio capture (also add what you are not doing, eg all shots from static positions – no drone).

10 Client materials/assets required:

Brand guidelines, logos, content to be incorporated in experience, product information/descriptions. You can have deadlines here too.

GLOSSARY

360 video Video that is captured in all directions, rather than a single, cropped composition. This video is often described as 360×180 degrees, ie 360 degrees horizontally by 180 degrees vertically. To be seen 'correctly', 360 video needs to be played back in a way that mitigates its distortion. This takes wrapping it around a virtual sphere in a headset or in a desktop or online player such as YouTube or Facebook. 360 videos can be either stereoscopic or monoscopic.

algorithmic stitching Cameras like Google's Jump and the Jaunt One are designed to be stitched on the cloud, ie you upload the content to Google or Jaunt and they send you back stitched footage at a later time. This stitching is based on a series of ever-evolved algorithms that match the number of cameras and their specific orientation. It is fairly good most of the time, but when it comes back with issues then you've got a pretty painful process of trying to make a better job out of the 16-odd cameras of footage!

ambisonic audio For the purposes of VR film capture, ambisonics are a full-sphere audio-capture technique, often using dedicated ambisonic microphones such as the Sennheiser Ambeo. These microphones are then augmented with other directional mics and lav mics, picking up key pieces of audio from the whole scene. This technique gives far greater flexibility and control when going into audio post-production.

AR – augmented reality overlaying data, animations, content on to the real world. The longer game is to greatly increase our efficiency as humans, empowering our interpersonal communications, our understanding and interaction of the world, through navigation, health and safety, education – think the Terminator's view but a lot less fatal! Augmented reality apps have been given a boost recently with the release of ARKit and ARCore on iOS and Android respectively, allowing smartphones to sense their environments, understand the world around them and allow you to interact.

binaural audio Audio that is recorded and/or played back in a way that reproduces the way the human ear will hear it. Quite literally, bi means two and aural means ears. In theory, if you use a microphone, built/shaped like a human head, you can capture sound that will more realistically create the 'correct' sound of a given scene. However, we find that it is often not the best way to capture the audio, rather, it is better to capture the audio with ambisonics but let the playback in the app be optimized for binaural.

Cardboard This is Google Cardboard, the cheap, DIY VR headset from Google, often just referred to as 'Cardboard' in the industry. Google Cardboard headsets are not made by Google, but follow a set of design instructions established by them. There are more Google Cardboard headsets in the market than any other VR headset; however, they are often only used for a single experience and then discarded.

comfort In VR this specifically refers to whether an experience makes the user feel nauseous. Not only does a nauseous experience break the spell of presence, it also stays with the user for a long time after trying the content. Not something you want people associating with your brand!

equirectangular The projection of a 360 video when laid flat or in edit, this is the 'native' projection of the video and carries a lot of visible distortion. It is often used in films/TV in this projection to give the feel of an altered reality, eg Altered Carbon. The ratio of the projection is 2×1 or 360×180, as opposed to 16×9.

foveated rendering This is the idea that you can maintain a higher resolution on only the exact area of vision that is being looked at at any moment, the other parts in the peripheral of the view will be lower resolution and focus. In many respects this mimics how the eye works in the real world and in theory means greater resolution at a lower cost in processor power and componentry.

game engine Also known as a 'real-time' engine, this is the system that powers a computer game or interactive, heavily graphic-based experience. These are typically one of two 'engines', either Unity or Unreal. Both of these systems allow programmers to make virtual worlds with varying amounts of interactivity. At Visualise, we built a VR piece for *Wired* called 'The Cell', which combined a real-time games engine – Unity, with full body-motion tracking from Viacom. The game engine rendered the graphics and audio into the experience, taking the real-time data from the motion capture system so that people could look at their hands and feet and see the body of a robot! Game engines allow for interactivity in VR, and will enable future VR experiences that are based on 3D scanning real locations or events live.

interactive VR Virtual reality experiences that are built on a 'game engine' and allow you, the user, to impact the environment or the outcome of events. This could be anything from The Void's *Star Wars* experiences featuring interactive real-world objects and guns through to simple museum VR apps such as the one we produced for the Van Gogh Museum and Facebook.

lightfield cameras These are cameras that capture content from an area, rather than a single point, thereby allowing the user 'six degrees of freedom' (6DOF), ie they can move their body, lean left, right, up, down, to a limited degree, greatly increasing the sense of presence.

monoscopic The term used to describe a 360 video that looks flat, ie it has no depth to it. Few cameras can shoot 360 in 3D (stereoscopic), the majority shoot in monoscopic. For online uses such as Facebook and YouTube you will not see the difference, it is only on VR headsets that you see the huge benefit and reality that 3D brings to content.

MR – mixed reality I think this is a marketing term (Jonathan Waldern agrees; see the interview in the Introduction). Microsoft 'mixed reality' headsets are virtual reality headsets, they use sensors on the front of them to track the environment, but only to allow you to explore the virtual space. There is some argument that there is an obscure form of content that is sometimes referred to as 'hybrid reality' and encompasses a virtual environment that perfectly mimics real-world objects that also exist in the real world in the same place at the same time... No direct application for now in marketing!

nadir The bottom of a sphere, therefore, what you see when you look down in a 360 video.

optical flow A method of stitching that does not just apply a best-guess template to aligning videos on a seam, but rather looks at the objects in the scene and tries to manipulate the images to match. Nine times out of ten this leaves a seamless stitch, but sometimes it looks a lot worse! Optical flow was purely for high-end, and expensive platform's like the Foundry's Cara VR, but new entrants to the market like SGO's Mistika have democratized optical flow stitching.

photogrammetry The technique of building a 3D model of the real world using hundreds or thousands of photos of a space taken at multiple different angles and positions. The resulting model has unparalleled realism to it. One of the main drawbacks though is that it only captures a static environment, you cannot have people, etc. This is a form of 'volumetric capture'.

presence The complete connection of a VR user to the virtual world, getting lost or engrossed in the content. Forgetting the real world and being perfectly in tune with the virtual. Somewhat of a universal objective for brand-based VR.

SLAM (simultaneous logging and mapping) The computer or mobile device's ability to detect its environment and dynamically keep its position updated so that it can overlay content on to it or interpret that environment for something like automated driving. Effectively it is the device's way of mapping and interpreting the real world, mostly used in AR rather than VR.

Steam The games platform that works on Mac or PC, allows for HTC Vive and Oculus headsets to be used with VR-enabled games.

stereoscopic (3D) The term used to describe a 360 video that is shot with depth, ie each eye is seeing the scene from a slightly different angle. Very effective when used in 360 video, standard on interactive VR. Shooting in stereoscopic brings more challenges in post-production – it produces a video that has both the left eye and the right eye in one frame (typically left eye on top and right eye below). This is double the amount of data.

stitching The process of blending videos shot from a 360 video camera. The camera typically has between two and six lenses, each recording their own videos. These videos all need to be aligned, overlapping each other, and then carefully blended together so that the intersection between videos becomes invisible and the stitch 'seamless'. Not always possible, but far more as the technology is developing!

Swayze effect A term used to describe the feeling of being invisible in VR, feeling part of the scene but being unable to effect it, like Patrick Swayze in the motion picture *Ghost*. The Swayze effect can be mitigated by interaction with the scene, hence interactive VR does not tend to be effected, or by having actors looking at the camera and talking to 'you' breaking the fourth wall.

volumetric capture A way of capturing an entire space/moment from every conceivable angle, allowing the resulting footage to be experienced in VR so that you can walk around the content. Light field cameras are a form of volumetric capture, as is photogrammetry.

VR – virtual reality A real or imagined environment that has been captured or created for either interactive or passive consumption on a wearable headset. A complete takeover of your senses.

VRcades Arcades for virtual reality content, ie gaming zones where you can come and pay to play immersive content. Popular at present in China and the United States.

zenith The top of a sphere, therefore, what you see when you look up in a 360 video.

INDEX

NB: page numbers in *italic* indicate figures or tables.